WEEKEND WARRIORS
From Tyne To Tweed

WEEKEND WARRIORS

WARRIORS

From Tyne to Tweed

T.L. HEWITSON

TEMPUS

Front cover photograph: *3rd (Militia) Battalion NF lodging colours in Alnwick Castle, July 1908. They are formed up in the inner bailey with the record tower in the background. (D. Wood)*

Frontispiece: *9th RNF TA Machine Gun Battalion of 18 Division, firing a concentration shoot. The battalion went into captivity under the Japanese at Singapore, 16 February 1942.*

First published 2006

Tempus Publishing Limited
The Mill, Brimscombe Port,
Stroud, Gloucestershire, GL5 2QG
www.tempus-publishing.com

© T.L. Hewitson, 2006

The right of T.L. Hewitson to be identified as the Author
of this work has been asserted in accordance with the
Copyrights, Designs and Patents Act 1988.

British Library Cataloguing in Publication Data.
A catalogue record for this book is available from the British Library.

ISBN 0 7524 3756 9

Typesetting and origination by Tempus Publishing Limited
Printed in Great Britain

CONTENTS

Introduction 7

Acknowledgements 10

Abbreviations 12

one The Northumberland Militia: 'The Northumberland Buffs' 15

two The Revolutionary and Napoleonic Wars 1793–1815 41

three The Northumberland Hussar Yeomanry: 'The Noodles' 59

four The Rifle Volunteers 81

five The Artillery Volunteers 101

six The Engineer Volunteers 115

seven The Territorial Force 1908–1918 123

eight The Territorial Army 1920–1945 141

nine The Territorial Army 1947–1967 159

ten The New Territorials 1967–2004 175

Select Bibliography 187

Unit Index 189

Field kitchen in 1964. 1st (N) General Hospital RAMR. (Mytchett)

INTRODUCTION

For centuries Northumberland and Newcastle-upon-Tyne were the scenes of ruthless border raids and bloody wars. When the Romans arrived they eventually built Hadrian's Wall, eighty Roman miles long, from the Solway to the Tyne, which the author David Devine labelled the 'North West Frontier of Rome' in his *Military Study of Hadrian's Wall* (London, 1969). But Hadrian put the people north of the Tyne on the wrong side of the wall! Consequently, when the Antonine Wall was built in the lowlands of Scotland it effectively created a no man's land – a land between.

After the Normans arrived there was continual fighting along the border, with both sides claiming ownership. There was further conflict after the northern barons' revolt against King John in 1215, and the Scottish King Alexander came down with an army and received the homage of the barons at Felton in Northumberland. Rather displeased, King John came up from the south with an army, laid waste to the countryside and burnt Alnwick. For 300 years from the late thirteenth century onwards, there was constant war between the Scots and the English. This explains the abundance of castles, towers, and fortified farmhouses in the area. Berwick-on-Tweed changed hands numerous times; Newcastle was occupied by the Scots on more than one occasion. When we were not fighting the Scots we were fighting amongst ourselves. The Reivers from across the border, and from Redesdale and Tynedale, stole cattle, murdered, raped and pillaged throughout the north. The last attempt by the Scots to gain the throne of England was Bonnie Prince Charlie's abortive uprising in 1745.

During all this time the people of the area were more or less left to defend themselves. So it is little wonder that the people of the North East have become an independent-minded, bluntly spoken, dour, stoical and stubborn race apart. As a Yorkshire officer who served with a Territorial Battalion of the Northumberland Fusiliers during the First World War put it:

They are not as a whole a quick or very intelligent race. But for stark grim courage under the most awful surroundings they stand second to none. There is a streak of ruthlessness, too, in their dealings with the enemy; a legacy from the old Border Wars with the Scots. They are quite ready, if need be, to take no prisoners. A hard and strong, but lovable race of men.

These qualities inspired the defence correspondent of *The Times* to write a report on 17 July 1953 on Exercise *Water Scorpion*, the first full-scale divisional exercise held in Great Britain after the end of the Second World War, which gave a glowing account of the conduct of 50th (Northumbrian) Division (TA). His closing comments summed up the calibre of the Territorial soldiers of the north-east in those days and, I believe, are still just as relevant today:

… A Territorial formation which has won a great reputation over the last ten days – with a performance which could be compared at times with that of an active division of the Army of the Rhine … the divisional and brigade headquarters companies had been properly trained … the artillery won warm praise from several quarters … the infantry have moved and fought, by day and night with remarkable spirit and dug ferociously. One will carry away a special feeling of admiration for the 5th West Yorkshires, the 6th Durham Light Infantry, and the 7th Royal Northumberland Fusiliers, but almost everywhere these north-countrymen whether National Servicemen or volunteers, looked (and on occasion grumbled) like formidable soldiers. They inherited, of course, a great tradition; they have had 10,000 men in camp; most belong, by birth, to a hard fighting breed.

This expression of the quality of the Territorials indicated that they were maintaining the pride and spirit of those who had gone before them, a tradition which, I believe, continues in the men and women serving today. As long as this country can still produce citizens who are willing to give their time and dedication, and have pride in themselves and their country, we still have a chance to maintain our freedom and democracy. Patriotism, loyalty and a belief in the democratic system are sentiments much derided today in our politically correct society which seems to me to be trying to make us ashamed to be British – and appears to be succeeding. Whether these sentiments can be upheld in the face of the anti-British politicians, of all parties, who administer our country today, aided by the liberal left, is something that we may have no control over in the future.

After the events of 11 September 2001, when terrorism entered a new dimension, governments of the western world have had to come to terms with problems of domestic defence. These events caused Geoff Hoon, the New Labour Defence Minister, to admit in the *Daily Telegraph* on 20 February 2002, that, 'he was glad that the TA had not been fully cut from its previous strength of 56,000 to 41,200 set by the defence review'. He further stated, 'it was a bit of luck that the Strategic Defence Review – the 1998 revamp of Britain's armed forces – had not been fully implemented'. However, in the latest review (2004/2005) it would seem that New Labour politicians are continuing with the old socialist tradition of reducing the defence budget, thus reducing the operational capability of our armed forces. And yet, the Prime Minister seems to be committing the armed forces more and more to operational roles while simultaneously reducing their numbers. It is possible that the politicians may place our whole national defence system in jeopardy with their false economies. They do so at our peril.

Lt Darling (left) and Lt Robertson (right), Berwick Artillery Vols, c.1880.

ACKNOWLEDGEMENTS

There are many people to whom I owe a debt for their assistance with this account. If I miss some of them by default, I apologise profusely. Without the aid of the Sir James Knott Trust this work may never have come to fruition. I would like to thank Colonel Charles Baker-Cresswell for his support over the years in my research into the military history of Northumberland and its soldiers; my long-time friend Major (Rtd) Dennis Thornton for his contribution with his computer skills; Dyllis Harding, Anna Flowers and all the staff of the local studies department in Newcastle Central Library for permission to use archive material from the library collections; Sue Wood and all the staff of the County Record Office at Gosforth, and Linda Bankier of Berwick-upon-Tweed Record Office for permission to use document BRO 128; The Army Museums Ogilby Trust, and the National Archives for permission to use material from their collections; His Grace The Duke of Northumberland, Claire Baxter and Sarah Darling of Northumberland Estates, for permission to use images of items in the collections in Alnwick Castle; the staff of the National Army Museum.

I would like to thank Colonel Denis Wood for permission to use his photographs; the adjutants of the various TA units throughout Tyne to Tweed, who have given me so much assistance; Major (Rtd) Joe Foster, formerly Permanent Staff Administration Officer of 'Z' (Fusilier) Company, The Tyne Tees Regiment (TA), for permission to use his photographs; Captain (Rtd) Tony Boyd, PSAO of 'Z' Company and Ian Souter for their assistance with photographs; Staff Sergeant Michael Thornton, The Royal Army Medical Corps, and Fred Redpath for their photographs; my old friend Jim Winter for his encouragement, photographs and knowledge; David I. Moore for the use of his superb photographs of the Berwick Artillery and Rifle Volunteers; Ray Middleton for his photographs, generosity and friendship; Ralph Jackson for his photographs; Ralph Thompson of the Northumberland Hussars Museum, also for the use of photographs; Mrs Ann Alexander for permission to use images of the military paintings of my great friend, her late husband James Alexander.

My thanks to Brigadier N.G.R. Hepworth, and Major (Rtd) F. Calvert of the Reserve Forces and Cadet Association for the North of England for permission to use images from their collection; The Trustees of the Fusilier Museum of Northumberland for permission to quote from the *St George's Gazette,* the former regimental journal of The Royal Northumberland Fusiliers, a unique unbroken record of the activities of the regiment from 1883 to 1968, when it was amalgamated into The Royal Regiment of Fusiliers. Extracts from the Delaval manuscripts reproduced by kind permission jointly of Newcastle Central Library and Northumberland County Archives Services. Finally to my wife and daughter my thanks for their support and understanding.

ABBREVIATIONS

Ack-ack: Anti-Aircraft.
ACC: Army Catering Corps.
ACF: Army Cadet Force.
AGRA: Army Group Royal Artillery.
ASCV: Army Service Corps Volunteers.
ATS: Auxiliary Territorial Army.
Bty: Battery.
CB: Companion of the Order of the Bath.
CBE: Commander of the Order of the British Empire.
DCM: Distinguished Conduct Medal.
DL: Deputy Lieutenant.
DSO: Distinguished Service Order.
GC: George Cross.
GCB: Grand Cross of the Order of the Bath.
GH: Green Howards.
GM: George Medal.
GS: General Service.
GT: General Transport.
HAA: Heavy Anti-Aircraft.
HDF: Home Defence Force.
HG: Home Guard.
HM: His or Her Majesty.
JP: Justice of the Peace.
KCMG: Knight Commander of the Order of Saint Michael & Saint
                 George
KBE: Knight Commander of the Order of the British Empire.
KG: Knight of the Order of the Garter.
KOSB :   King's Own Scottish Borderers.
LAA: Light Anti-Aircraft.
LAD: Light Aid Detachment.

LDV:	Local Defence Volunteers.
LI:	Light Infantry.
LF:	Lancashire Fusiliers.
MBE:	Member of the Order of the British Empire.
MC:	Military Cross.
MM:	Military Medal.
MP:	Member of Parliament.
MT:	Motor Transport.
NAV:	Newcastle Artillery Volunteers.
NAAFI:	Navy, Army & Air Force Institute.
NF:	Northumberland Fusiliers.
NRV:	Newcastle Rifle Volunteers.
NH:	Northumberland Hussars.
NM:	Northumberland Militia.
NAV:	Northumberland Artillery Volunteers.
NAM:	Northumberland Artillery Militia.
NRGAV:	Northumberland Royal Garrison Artillery Volunteers.
NCO:	Non-Commissioned Officer.
NRO:	Northumberland Record Office.
OBE:	Officer of the Order of the British Empire.
OTC:	Officers Training Corps.
PAV:	Percy Artillery Volunteers.
PRV:	Percy Rifle Volunteers.
QOY:	Queen's Own Yeomanry.
RA:	Royal Artillery.
RAC:	Royal Armoured Corps.
RAAF:	Royal Auxiliary Air Force.
RAF:	Royal Air Force.
RAMC:	Royal Army Medical Corps.
RAOC:	Royal Army Ordnance Corps.
RASC:	Royal Army Service Corps.
RCT:	Royal Corps of Transport.
RE:	Royal Engineers.
RECCE:	Reconnaissance Corps.
REME:	Royal Electrical & Mechanical Engineers.
RF:	Royal Fusiliers.
RLC:	Royal Logistic Corps.
RMP:	Royal Military Police.
RMR:	Royal Marine Reserve.
RNF:	Royal Northumberland Fusiliers.

RNR: Royal Naval Reserve.
RNVR: Royal Naval Volunteer Reserve.
RRF: Royal Regiment of Fusiliers.
RS: Royal Signals.
RTC: Royal Tanks Corps.
RTR: Royal Tank Regiment.
RVC: Rifle Volunteer Corps.
SAS: Special Air Service.
Sqn: Squadron.
TA: Territorial Army.
TAER: Territorial Army Emergency Reserve.
TAV: Tynemouth Artillery Volunteers.
TAVR: Territorial Army Volunteer Reserve.
TD: Territorial Decoration.
TEE: Tyne Electrical Engineers.
TEM: Territorial Efficiency Medal.
TF: Territorial Force.
TSM: Tynemouth Submarine Miners.
VB: Volunteer Battalion.
VD: Volunteer Decoration.
Warwicks: Royal Warwickshire Fusiliers.

ONE

THE NORTHUMBERLAND MILITIA: 'THE NORTHUMBERLAND BUFFS'

On the twenty-fourth the route to us came,
For bonny Newcastle we march our brave corps.
The streets will be crowded, the people will cry,
'Here comes the Newcastle glittering by'

J. Bell, Newcastle, 1814.

According to Major Adamson in *Services of the Northumberland Light Infantry Militia* (Newcastle, 1877), the first documentary evidence relating to the Northumberland Militia relates to an Act of Parliament of 1662, [13th Charles 2nd, Chap. 3rd] for ordering out the forces of the several counties in the Kingdom. The complement to be found in Northumberland was:

Light Horse, furnished by Peers, called the Lords Horse.

The Duke of Northumberland	2
Earl of Northumberland	6
Earl of Carlisle	3
Lord Grey	10
Lord Widdrington	2
Lord Derwentwater	4
Total:	27

Every gentleman was charged according to his estate, the proportion being:

1	Baronet-Sir Ralph Delaval	3
121	other gentlemen	48
128	Lords and gentlemen, Light Horse	78

Very little documentary evidence of Northumberland Militia activity in the late seventeenth and early eighteenth century seems to exist for the above, and the 1745 Hexham militia rolls for the North Tyne, South Tyne and Hexham companies (200 names by company) held in Northumberland County Record Office [ZAL. 98/5]. There was also the headstone of Edward Bell of Eachwick, in Northumberland, buried in St John's Newcastle, who at the time of his death in 1743 held the rank of Major in the county militia. So it seems to have been in existence.

Until the Militia Act of 1757 (George II. cap 25.) – 'An act for the better ordering out of the Militia Forces in the several counties of that part of Great Britain called England' – liability for providing men fell upon individual land and property owners. After the 1775 Act came into force, each county or parish became liable to provide a set quota of men for the general militia. They were selected by ballot from lists prepared by local magistrates acting on information given by householders of all males between eighteen and thirty who resided in their homes.

The militia was not expected to serve overseas. It was to be used for home defence and as an aid to the civil power. All the organisation and administration of each county militia was under the jurisdiction of the Lord Lieutenant who was responsible to the Home Office. It was he who authorised the local magistrates to instigate the annual ballot, or after a state of emergency had been declared. He was also empowered by the Sovereign to grant commissions in the militia to those who qualified under property regulations. Deputy Lieutenants and Colonels were to have incomes of £400 per annum, or be heirs to twice that amount; Lieutenant Colonels and Majors, £300; Captains, £200; Lieutenants, £100; and Ensigns, £50 per annum.

Unless a state of emergency or war existed, the only obligation of a selected person was to undertake annual training of a specified length. In the case of the Northumberland Militia the muster was normally held at Alnwick. However, there were exceptions. A person could pay a substitute to take his place, and it was generally recognised that, in essence, the militia was an army of substitutes. If a Quaker, or other non-conformist, was chosen, and refused to serve or provide a substitute, the Deputy Lieutenant would provide one and levy the cost on the person in question.

After the 1775 Act, the 560 men of the Northumberland were embodied in 1759 by virtue of an Act of Parliament passed by George II, authorising the raising of the militia for the different counties. A list of officers dated 15 August 1759 shows:

Sir Edward Blacket, Bart., Colonel.
George Delaval Esq., Lieutenant Colonel.
Sir Matthew White, Bart., Major.
Captain Abraham Dixon.
Lieutenant Thomas Wood, Beadnel.
Ensign William Pratt, Warenton.
Captain Christopher Reed, Chipchase.
Lieutenant Henry Tulip. Fallowfield.
Ensign William Stokoe, Chollerton.
Captain John Hall, Whitely.
Ensign John Stephenson, North Shields.
Ensign Charles Barker, Earsdon.
Captain William Ward, Morpeth.
Lieutenant William Ord, Morpeth.
Ensign William Fenwick, Alnwick.
Captain John Dawson, Brunton.
Lieutenant Francis Dawson. Newcastle.
Ensign Henry Fenwick, Hexham.
Captain William Ord, -?-.
Lieutenant Edward Hall, North Shields.
Ensign Thomas Rutherford, Whitley.
Captain Alexander Collingwood, Unthank.
Lieutenant Edward Adams, Alnwick.
Ensign William Reed, -?-.
Captain Stephen Watson, North Seaton.
Lieutenant Thomas Newton, Hawkswell.
Ensign Anthony Proctor, Morpeth.

NEWCASTLE OFFICERS
Captain John Erasmus Blackett.
Lieutenant Edward Mosely.
Ensign Robert Stephenson.

BERWICK OFFICERS
Captain Gabriel Selby, Paston.
Lieutenant William Burrell, Howtel.
Ensign George Archbold, Alnwick.
Adjutant John Evans.

The militia was embodied, or mobilised, for part of the Seven Years' War (1756–1763), from 25 February 1760 until December 1762, when it was disembodied, or demobilised. During this period it was stationed at Berwick. Militia service was never popular with the people and in the eighteenth and early nineteenth centuries there were frequent riots over the balloting of individuals. Another factor in the unpopularity of the militia was the cost incurred by the parishes maintaining the families of militiamen during annual training and wartime mobilisation. As a result of this discontent a serious riot occurred at Hexham, of which a full account is given in *Richardson's Table Book*, Vol. 2. On Monday 9 March 1761, the Deputy Lieutenants and Justices of the Peace acting for Tindale Ward, met at Hexham to receive the lists of those liable to serve in the militia. As a result of the justices having heard that a number of people were going to try and prevent the lists being delivered, six companies of the North York Militia were marched from Newcastle and formed three sides of a hollow square in the Market Place, the fourth side being the Town Hall.

Between 10 and 11 a.m., a crowd of about 5,000, armed with weapons of all sorts, congregated. They claimed that if the ballot was not suspended, they would murder the magistrates. They also tried to bribe the militia to lay down their arms. Eventually, at 1 p.m., the Riot Act was read. The rioters then tried to break through the ranks of the militia. In the mêlée, Ensign Hart was killed by a shot from a pistol. The militia were ordered to open fire into the crowd. As a result fifty-one of the rioters were killed and 300 wounded. Two of them, Peter Patterson and William Elder, were arrested and charged with High Treason and later sentenced at the County Assizes:

> To be drawn upon a hurdle to the place of execution on Wednesday, the 30th September next, and then severally hanged by the neck, to be severally cut down, and have their entrails taken out and burnt before their faces; to have their heads severed from their bodies, and their bodies afterwards severally divided into four quarters, and their quarters disposed of at His Majesty's pleasure.

On 5 October, Peter Paterson was executed at Morpeth. William Elder's execution was held back for a year, then he was pardoned. After the events that had occurred in Hexham Market Place, the North York Militia were nicknamed 'The Hexham Butchers'. Allan Hind, in his *History of Northumberland,* Vol. 3 (pp. 258–259), claims that Peter Patterson was not even in Hexham at the time of the riot.

These events did not stop the balloting taking place. A report in the *Newcastle Journal*, 12 June 1762, states:

> We hear that tomorrow, in the forenoon, copies of the lists of all persons resident in the several Parishes of this Town, liable to serve in the Militia, will be affixed to the respective Church doors, and that the said lists will be returned to the Deputy Lieutenants, at the

Guild Hall, in the same town, on Friday next, the 18th inst., at ten o'clock in the forenoon, when all persons who shall think themselves aggrieved by having their names inserted in such lists, or by any other being omitted, may appeal and that no appeal will be afterwards received.

There was also trouble with the substitutes as many of them took the money paid to them by the person they were substituting for, and then disappeared. An advertisement in the *Newcastle Journal*, 8 March 1760, advised:

This is to give notice that William Clay, born at Sunderland by the Sea, the County of Durham, aged about 26 years, five feet four inches, by trade a STAYMAKER, a little pitted with smallpox, a little white looking, was inrolled [sic] in Captain John Hall's Company of the Militia, for the County of Northumberland, in the month of September 1757, and was working at his trade in Durham in 1759, and has not since been heard of. If the said William Clay be alive, and will report to Captain John Hall at Berwick upon Tweed, or to the said James Bell, at North Shields, within one month from the date hereof, he shall be kindly received; or if any person will give notice to Captain Hall, or the said James Bell, where the said William Clay is (if still alive, or of the time of his death, and where he is buried, if dead) shall receive one guinea [£1.05] for their trouble, and all reasonable charges will be paid.

On 26 March 1778, an order was issued to the Duke of Northumberland, Lord Lieutenant of Northumberland, to embody the regiment, stating that 'warlike preparations in France become every day more considerable'. Accordingly, the regiment assembled at Alnwick on 13 April. After marching to Newcastle, three companies remained in billets in the town, and the others marched to Tynemouth Barracks. An extra company was raised in Newcastle by an Edward Dale, assisted by the Corporation; he was gazetted Captain. A bounty of 10 guineas (£10.50) was paid to anyone enlisting in the company for three years, 5 guineas (£5.25) on signing, and another 5 guineas on joining. The regiment later marched to Beverly in Yorkshire, then Hull. The London *Daily Advertiser,* 29 May 1778, had a report headed: 'Leeds 26 May. Lord Algernon Percy, Colonel of the Northumberland Militia, has ordered, at his own expense, every private in the regiment a buff–coloured waistcoat and breeches, a pair of Guetres [sic: Gaiters] and shoe buckles'. Hence the nickname 'Northumberland Buffs'.

On 19 May 1780, they marched for London. They arrived at Holborn on Wednesday 7 June, after a day's march of 40 miles. The regiment immediately became involved in aid to the civil power duties, playing a major part in putting down the anti-Catholic Gordon Riots in the City of London. The rioters, led by Lord George Gordon, who called his movement the 'Protestant Association', held London at their mercy for nearly a week and engaged in an orgy of murder and destruction. Their cause was unashamed religious prejudice. The aim was to repeal the Catholic Relief Bill which had been passed with the support of the government and opposition in 1778. The *Scots' Magazine*, July 1780, reported:

At about 11 p.m. on 7 June, a party of the Northumberland Militia came into Holborn; they had marched that day nearly 40 miles, and the moment they arrived at their place of rendezvous, which was Lincoln's Inn Fields, they were sent into Holborn. As soon as they appeared before the bonfire in front of Mr. Langdale's house, the insurgents attacked them. The party then discharged their pieces [muskets], but as they were only loaded with powder no harm was done; this experiment was tried to intimidate the ruffians, for strict orders had been given to use every measure before coming to extremity, but it had no effect. The insurgents continued their attack, and one of the officers being very much hurt, it was found absolutely necessary to fire with ball; yet the fire was very prudently conducted, for the soldiers were not permitted to fire along the street. Their officers drew them up along the north side of Holborn, fronting the bonfire and the house on fire, so that no person could be hurt but those who were rioting around the fire burning the furniture and casks, and those who were still in the house plundering it. By the second volley two or three were killed. This conduct of the officers deserves great praise, for the streets were much crowded by people moving their most valuable goods, as they did not know where the fire would stop. No innocent person could suffer by the firing, for it went across the bonfire into the house. The second had the proper effect and drove off the insurgents from the front of the houses, but many rioters and plunderers were still within, the fire not yet having reached the front of the house. When any of these appeared at the doors and windows, the soldiers on the flank of the party came up in Indian file; that is. Each man singly following the back of the first to the doors and windows and gave their fire, each man falling off as he fired.

As a gesture of appreciation of the conduct of the regiment, the inhabitants of Lincoln's Inn Fields subscribed £59 17s (£59.85) for the benefit of the soldiers. However, it was not only the militiamen who were involved. The *Newcastle Journal*, 24 June 1780, tells us that:

When the Northumberland Militia were placed in Lincoln's Inn, for the defence of the place during the late riots, the soldier's wives and their children were excluded, and exposed to great hardships at so distressing a juncture, on which Mr Ward, of Staples Inn, a gentleman of property in Northumberland [Stannington], waited on Lord Algernon Percy, the Colonel, where he found Lord Loughborough, and represented to them the cruel situation of the poor women, adding that he would accommodate 20 or 30 in the Hall of Staples Inn, and requested that the rest be distributed in like manner amongst among the different Halls of the Inns of Court. Upwards of 90, however, were sent to Mr Ward, who has ever since sustained them at his own expense, with buttocks of beef and cabbage.

Alnwick Castle.

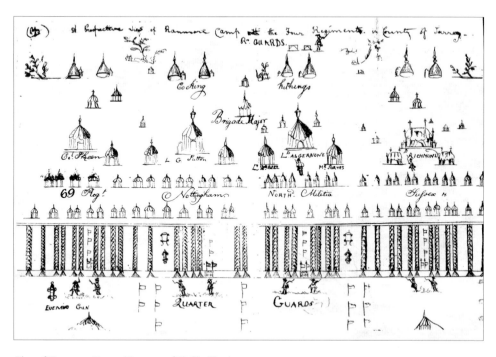

Plan of Ranmoor Camp. (Courtesy of Ogilby Trust)

Mr Ward was obviously a generous and humane man with a social conscience. The regiment was next encamped with Nottingham, and Sussex Militias and the 69th Regiment of Foot, at Ranmoor Camp, Dorking, in Surrey.

> *To Ranmoor camp we marched away,*
> *This was our inclination,*
> *And there in readiness we lay,*
> *For to defend our nation;*
> *If France or Spain attempt to land,*
> *Our guns shall roar like thunder,*
> *By flesh and blood, and all that's good,*
> *We'll make these dogs knock under.*

By 1782 the regiment was in winter quarters at Southampton. They later moved to Chatham, and then marched back to Northumberland where they were disembodied in December of that year. Another period of full-time service began when the militia were again embodied at Alnwick on Thursday 3 January 1793, as a result of the outbreak of the French Revolutionary Wars. The years 1793 to 1796 were spent moving around Durham, Yorkshire and Cumberland. In 1796 they marched south, eventually going into barracks at Colchester. The conduct of some of the men seems to have been rather disorderly. As a result, the sentences of Courts Martial during this period were very severe. A private being absent from morning parade was awarded 100 lashes; another for being drunk on morning parade, 150 lashes. For being insolent to his captain on marching to evening parade, a private was given 300 lashes. In October 1795 a private was charged with being drunk and striking a corporal of the guard, for which he was given 400 lashes. On 6 March 1797 another private was given 500 lashes for being absent without leave. Strict discipline was obviously maintained by a forceful and brutal regime.

After a strenuous few years during which time they marched around half of England, by June 1798 the regiment, 1,300 strong, was at Hornsea. The men were employed protecting the crops and assisting with the harvest. An incident reported in the *Newcastle Courant*, 13 October 1798, mentions an accident involving the family of a militiaman while they were on the march from Hornsea Camp to Bridlington: 'A baggage wagon of the Northumberland Militia broke down, or overturned, by which a poor woman had both her thighs broken, and her two children were killed on the spot.'

In 1798 Charles William Bigge appears as Lieutenant Colonel Commandant of the Northumberland Supplemental Militia, which was designated as the 2nd Battalion. In September this battalion marched from Alnwick, through

Newcastle, to Sunderland Barracks. During August and September 1797 they were at South Shields. The battalion was disembodied at Clifford's Fort, North Shields, in November 1799.

An order was given in 1799 for one quarter of the regiment to volunteer into the regular army, and 266 privates transferred. 132 went to the 17th Foot, seventy-six to the 56th Foot and six to the Royal Artillery. The 5th Foot and the 52nd Foot received the remainder. After another three years of marching and counter-marching from Northern England to Southern England, and back again, the regiment was ordered to be disembodied due to the Peace of 1802 being agreed with France, having been nine years and five months on active service.

After marching via Hull, Beverly, Pocklington, York, Easingwold, Thirsk, Northallerton, Darlington and Durham, the regiment arrived in Newcastle on Wednesday 17 April 1802. The *Newcastle Courant* gave a fulsome account of the regiment's arrival:

> On Wednesday last, the first division of the Northumberland Militia, under the command of Colonel Reed, marched into this town from Hull. They were received on the [Tyne] Bridge with joyous acclimations, by a great concourse of people, and at the head of Dean Street the Newcastle Volunteers were drawn up, and saluted them with presented arms. The officers of the volunteers afterwards dined with Colonel Reed at Mr Charles Turner's inn [The Queens Head] where the day was spent in great conviviality and harmony. It is now nearly ten years since the Northumberland Regiment left their native county, in which time they have traversed a considerable part of England, and everywhere been distinguished for good appearance, discipline and behaviour. Another division arrived on Thursday. They are expected to march for Alnwick in a day or two to be disembodied.

The newspaper reporter had obviously not heard of the Courts Martial that had been held, and the punishments given.

Hostilities having recommenced with France, the regiment was embodied again on 22 April 1803. The numbers called up were 493 from Northumberland, 137 from Newcastle and 19 from Berwick, a total of 649. They spent the next two years in the North East. A local newspaper stated on 10 July 1805:

> The Northumberland Militia yesterday morning passed over Blackfriars Bridge in the course of their route from Sunderland Barracks to Chatham. They had their advance and rear guards, and where attended by an excellent band of music. They were in high spirits and seemed about 1,000 strong, and a finer regiment cannot be conceived. They were all young men, but of mature age and well made, and we have no doubt they are capable of beating an equal number of troops of any enemy in the world.

As the bulk of them were probably substitutes, for which the going rate was about £40, it is questionable whether they would they have been in such high spirits if they had known the extent of the march to the following destinations. They marched from Sunderland via Durham, Peterborough, Barnet, Highgate, Kentish Town, the City of London, Greenwich, Deptford, Rochester, Ospringe, and Canterbury, arriving at Margate Barracks in October, where they were detached on to anti-smuggling duties on the coast at Westdale, St Peter's, and Broadstairs. The years until 1810 were spent constantly on the move in the south of England. In that same year they relieved the Cornish Militia at Norman's Cross Barracks, guarding French Prisoners of War until October. Each member of the regiment subscribed one day's pay for the relief of British Prisoners of War in France. In 1811 the government intimated that they were sending regiments of the militia to Ireland. The Northumberland Regiment had twice offered to serve in Ireland during their embodiment. While stationed in Colchester Barracks, they volunteered once again. As a mark of distinction for offering their services, the regiment was converted to a light infantry role. Re-designated as The Northumberland Light Infantry Militia, their offer was accepted.

Sailing from Harwich, they arrived in Cork Cove, in Southern Ireland, on 22 August. The regiment had been embarked on three ships: 337 on the *Elisha Tupper*, 307 on the *Betsy*, and 316 on the *Martha*. One member of the regiment, Jeremy Knox, was not greatly impressed with conditions on board his particular ship. He wrote the words for a song, 'On the Northumberland Militia going to Ireland', and the following extract gives an indication of his disenchantment:

> *When I take a look round the vessel,*
> *And see the confusion and bother,*
> *That I ever left my poor mother;*
> *As for their allowance of victuals,*
> *I think they are damnably small,*
> *Before we accomplish our passage,*
> *I fear that our jaws they will fall.*

After garrison duties in various stations in the south of Ireland, the regiment returned to England and landed at Bristol on 11 October 1813. They then commenced a lengthy march to the North East, where they arrived on 15 November. Sykes' *Local Records*, Vol.2, and the local newspapers of the time, recorded the arrival of the regiment:

On November 15th and the following day, the Northumberland Militia passed through Newcastle on its route to Scotland. The van division of the regiment which was headed by

Lieutenant Colonel Coulson, was, on its entrance to the town , greeted with a salute of guns from the castle. The bells of St Nicholas Church rang a peal, and every demonstration of joy was displayed in compliment to the lads of [the] Coaly Tyne. The concourse of people that assembled to meet them was immense; Dean Street was completely blocked as they marched up. The regiment has not been in Newcastle for upwards of ten years.

SUB-DIVISION

OF

NEWCASTLE UPON TYNE

Instructions for Ballotted Men.

NO Seaman, Seafaring Man, Keelman, Waterman or any Man liable to be impressed into the Navy will be accepted as a Substitute.

Any other Man who may be offered as a Substitute on the Day of Inrolment, must produce a Certificate in Writing, under the Hand of the Clerk of the Sub-division in which he resides, or under the hand of the Constable of his Parish, Township, or Constablery, that his Name stands in the Ballot List, of the present Year.

The adjoining Parishes or Townships to Newcastle, are the following, viz .—

PARISHES—
- NEWBURN.
- RYTON.
- WHICKHAM.
- GATESHEAD.
- JARROW.
- TYNEMOUTH.
- WALLSEND.
- LONG BENTON.
- GOSFORTH.

TOWNSHIPS—
- BYKER.
- HEATON.
- JESMOND.
- FENHAM.
- ELSWICK.
- WESTGATE.
- BENWELL.

No Man will be accepted as a Substitute who does not dwell in Newcastle, or in some one of the above Parishes or Townships

March 26th 1831

J. Clark, Printer, 11, Newgate Street,

'Instructions for Balloted Men', 26 March 1831. (Courtesy of Newcastle Central Library)

On the direction of the mayor, each soldier was given 1s (5p) by the Corporation to drink His Majesty's health. The van division marched for Morpeth the next day and it was succeeded by the second division which received the same welcome. The next stage of their march took them to Scotland, arriving at Haddington on 24 November, where they wintered. They left Haddington on 18 February 1814, arriving back at Newcastle on 25 February. On 21 March they occupied Tynemouth Barracks, then on 21 June returned to Alnwick where they were disembodied on 24 June, having been eleven years and two months on active service. The number of men who volunteered into the Regular Army between the years 1805 and 1814 was 1,129 into Line Regiments, and 30 into the Royal Navy and Marines, making, with the 373 who had joined the army in 1799, a total of 1,532. From 1814 to 1819 there was no annual training. In 1820 the regiment was called out for twenty-eight days and once again there was trouble with deserters. Due to be called out again for twenty-one days on 3 July 1821, the Justices of the Peace placed an advertisement in the *Newcastle Courant,* of 3 March, with the names of twenty-four deserters, offering a reward of 20s (£1) for information about them, or a fine of £5 for harbouring them.

The annual training from 1825 to 1831 was intermittent, and after 1831 service with the militia, went into abeyance. However, the Militia Act of 1852 (15 & 16 Vict), designed, 'To consolidate and amend the laws regulating to the militia', radically changed the whole concept of militia service. The force was re-organised with a quota of 80,000 men to be raised nationally by voluntary enlistment, although the option of the ballot was retained by the government. A bounty of £6 was to be paid to men eighteen to thirty-five years of age, minimum height 5ft 4in, for five years' service. The training period was to be from twenty-one to fifty-six days annually. This Act also removed the administration of the militia from the Home Office to the War Office. But as the Lord Lieutenants in most counties were either in command of their County Militia, or directly connected with it, they still retained a degree of control.

This was the case with the Northumberland Militia, which was a particularly fashionable regiment. For many years, the local aristocracy, wealthy landowning families and business men of the Northumberland and Newcastle, were associated with it. It may have been that the association with the militia of the Duke of Northumberland and the Percy family, was a significant factor in the popularity of the regiment as far as the officers were concerned. Another was the fact that after the abolition of the purchase of commissions under the Regulation of the Forces Act of 1871, militia officers could transfer to the Regular Army without having to fulfil many of the qualifications laid down for the grant of a regular commission. For many of the other ranks who served in the militia the annual training would have been a diversion, particularly if they were unemployed. Training in the lush rural pastures of Alnwick, with regular meals plus pay, and a not too rigorous military regime, would have made a very welcome change for those who normally resided in the unhygienic and squalid conditions of the working-class districts of Newcastle, and the tied cottages in the rural areas of Northumberland in the mid- to late nineteenth century. It could only have had a beneficial effect upon them.

On 6 July 1853, the year after the service became voluntary, the 27th Northumberland Light Infantry Militia, as it was then titled, assembled for twenty-eight days' annual training at Alnwick, under the command of Lieutenant Colonel William Bigge, of Ovingham. His major was Lord Lovaine MP (later the 6th Duke of Northumberland). Due, perhaps, to the fact that service was now voluntary, 1,122 men had enlisted. However, only 850 reported for training. The Colonel of the Regiment was the Earl of Beverly, a member of the Percy family. He arrived in Alnwick on Saturday 16 July in time for the government inspecting officer to review the regiment on 19 July. The social standing of the officers of the regiment is evident by a report which appeared in the *Newcastle Journal*, Saturday 6 August 1854: 'A splendid ball was given by Colonel the Earl of Beverly and the officers, which was attended by about 300 of the elite of the ladies and gentlemen of the county'. A major international crisis affecting the militia was the Crimean War (1854–1856) which saw the regiment embodied on 9 January 1855. They remained in Alnwick until 5 September then marched to Tynemouth Barracks. They moved to Carlisle on 28 December. During this period, 395 men transferred to the Regular Army. On 24 May 1856 the regiment marched to Sunderland, returning to Alnwick on 16 June. They were disembodied four days later.

Thus we see another aspect of the militia, that of providing trained recruits for the army. But they were only adequately trained because of the length of time they had been on full-time service. In the normal course of events, with only twenty-eight days' annual training, and the units operating more or less independently, the militia would have been next to useless as a cohesive fighting force without a prolonged period of training. There was no annual training in 1857, but for the next ten years they trained at Alnwick, being billeted in the town, and the small barracks in Bondgate Without. By 1859 the enthusiasm for service in the militia seemed to have abated somewhat. The *Newcastle Courant*, 8 July, records that The Northumberland Light Infantry Militia had assembled at Alnwick for twenty-one days' training. Out of a potential strength of 900, just over 200 had reported there. The attitude of the North East Railway Co. may have exacerbated the situation. After the militia had been called out on 7 May 1861, a special train was laid on for the Newcastle men at the Central Station, bound for Alnwick. It seems that many of the men could not, or would not, pay the fare, and therefore the train was cancelled. Those who were able to pay went by the ordinary train, and those who were not, walked.

TO THE MEMORY OF
CAPTAIN ROBERT CRISP
UPWARDS OF THIRTY FIVE YEARS
ADJUTANT OF
THE NORTHUMBERLAND
REGIMENT OF MILITIA
WHO DIED THE 27TH DAY OF SEP. 1840,
AGED 72 YEARS.

THIS TABLET IS PLACED
AS A MEMORIAL OF HIS WORTH
AND OF THE ESTEEM
RESPECT AND REGRET
OF HIS
COMMANDING OFFICER.

Memorial in St Michael's church, Alnwick.
(J. Winter)

The regiment blotted its copybook in 1866. According to the local press, while off-duty, the militiamen were unruly and unmanageable. In one incident in that year they took possession of the police station and smashed a large number of house windows in the town, causing extensive damage. They may have been indulging themselves in Alnwick Castle Inn, Narrowgate Street, an establishment owned by Mrs Percy, prior to their vandalism. As her advertisement claimed:

> *When to the Castle Inn I went,*
> *To taste the noble PERCY cheer,*
> *I found the pies most excellent,*
> *And only equalled by the beer.*

A Mr Edward Allan of Alnwick, realising that there existed a large body of 'socially deprived' men in the town, decided that something should be done to provide them with some means of recreation and amusement that did not involve alcohol or women. As a result, with the aid of a committee of local people and the backing of the Duke of Northumberland, who was Colonel of the Regiment, a newsroom was established in the Town Hall. Here they were provided with newspapers and periodicals and the means to write home. So successful was this enterprise that larger premises had to be found. Consequently, the newsroom was moved to the Corn Exchange. As part of the scheme, subsidised by the Duchess of Northumberland, the men could buy a pint of tea or coffee and a penny loaf for 2*d*. Classes for teaching reading and writing were established and weekly concerts were arranged for the militiamen. These concerts became a feature of the annual training season and, according to an edition of *Alnwick Journal* in July 1872, the audiences of militiamen and local people numbered over 1,000. At that time it was a unique exercise in social engineering, copied by many other counties that had an annual influx of militiamen.

A spectacular event took place during the training period 1867, which commenced on 15 July and lasted for twenty-seven days. On 6 August, the Countess Percy presented a new set of colours to the regiment. This took place on the Pastures just below Alnwick Castle. From 1867 until 1871, the annual training was held at Alnwick for twenty-seven days on each occasion. The Army List for 1870 shows the Duke of Northumberland as Lieutenant Colonel of the Regiment. Several old county family names also appear on the list: Major John Mitford of Mitford; Captain Earl Percy, heir to the Dukedom; Captain Shalcross Widdrington; Lieutenant Alexander Browne of Callaly Castle. It was also in 1870 that evidence of aristocratic patronage manifested itself. This was the first year that a permanent camping site was established for the annual training, in accordance with new regulations superseding the billeting of troops in billets or lodgings. The tented camp was set up on the 'Little Havens', on the Pastures across the river Aln. It was reached via the Denwick Road from the town, south of the castle. Despite the public houses losing their income from billeting, they continued, no doubt, to be well patronised. There were still economic benefits for the other traders in the town. The militiamen had to be supplied with food and other essentials.

Remnants of 1867 'Queen's Colour' (Victoria) presented by Countess Percy and laid up in St Michael's church, Alnwick, in 1908, upon the regiment becoming part of Northumberland Fusiliers as 3rd Battalion. (J. Winter)

Annual Camp. Tented encampment on the pastures at Alnwick Castle, 1873. Note the white tunics of the bandsmen in the foreground.

In 1874 the Duke of Northumberland was appointed Honorary Colonel, with George Henry Grey as Lieutenant Colonel. Unfortunately, Grey died in the same year and the duke's son, Major, the Earl Percy, was appointed in his place. Another member of a prominent Northumberland family joined the militia at that time. He was O.C. Baker-Cresswell, who was promoted as major in 1875; he had formerly served as a captain in the 3rd Hussars. In that decade, several alterations were made to the dress and insignia of the regiment; collar badges consisting of a bugle and scroll were taken into wear.

A political crisis occurred in the East due to the war between Russia and Turkey (1877–1878). This led to the threat of war between Russia, and a coalition of European powers and Turkey. Warlike preparations were made by Disraeli's government, which included the mobilising of the militia reserve to report for regular army service by a Royal Warrant dated 30 April 1878. Out of a total strength of 239 reservists in the regiment, all but six reported to the headquarters at Alnwick. They were attached to the Regimental Depot of the 5th (Northumberland) Fusiliers at Ravensdowne Barracks, Berwick-upon-Tweed, then dismissed from service on 31 July. Helmets were taken into wear in this year, replacing the shakos previously worn by the officers. Annual training for the next three years was carried out on the Havens. Wide-ranging changes came into effect which were part of a radical programme of army modernisation instigated by Edward Cardwell, Secretary of State for War (1868–1874). As part of these measures, which became known as the 'Cardwell Reforms', regular, militia and volunteer battalions were amalgamated into territorial-based regiments with local designations and depots.

The Northumberland Light Infantry Militia was re-designated as the 3rd (Militia) Battalion, The Northumberland Fusiliers. The following changes were made to their uniforms:

1: Uniform facing colour: From buff to gosling green.
2: Lace: From silver to gold
3: Head dress: From helmet to fusilier fur cap,
4: Badges: Altered to Northumberland Fusiliers.

Nothing of great importance happened during the next few years, until 30 June 1890 when the battalion went by rail to Strensall Camp, York, for twenty-seven days' annual training. This was the first occasion since the Crimean War that the training was carried out away from Alnwick. In 1895 Colonel Earl Percy ADC retired from the battalion after thirty years' service, twenty of which he had been in command. Major Lord Algernon Percy was appointed Lieutenant Colonel as commanding officer. It can be seen that the command of the militia remained firmly in the hands of the Percy family. This could only have been of great benefit to the Northumberland Militia.

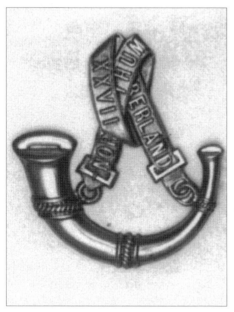

Above left: *Collar badge of the 27th Northumberland Light Infantry Militia. (D. Wood)*

Above right: *An officer's helmet plate, c.1880. In the centre is a blue velvet backing. Badge silver plate.
(D. Wood)*

The Boer War (1899–1902) was only the second time in the long history of the Northumberland Militia that it had served outside mainland Britain. On 12 December 1899, twenty-seven officers, thirty permanent staff and 355 militia soldiers assembled at Newcastle (Fenham) Barracks and proceeded by rail to Victoria Barracks, Portsmouth. This was a fortunate time to have wealthy aristocrats, landowners, sons of rich industrialists and businessmen as officers in the battalion, and it was then that another example of paternalism came into play. A separation allowance 8*d* [4p] was allowed by the government. The Northumberland and Tyneside Reservist Fund also assisted wives and families of embodied militiamen. These benefits were further enhanced by the militia officers who raised a substantial fund which granted to each man half the amount they voluntarily sent to their families. In the case of men proceeding to South Africa, where the remittance to families was obligatory, the officers granted the whole amount equal to the remittance. The 151 militia reservists of the 3rd Battalion embarked for South Africa on the SS *Jelunga*, together with 252 men of the 2nd Battalion of the regiment. Two sergeants and two corporals reverted to the rank of private so that they could embark. On 3 February 1900 the remainder of the battalion was embodied, and on 10 February they sailed on the SS *Pavonia*, for Malta.

A Special Army Order dated 17 February 1900 was received, informing the battalion that Her Majesty Queen Victoria (1819–1901) had approved the formation of two extra battalions, 3rd and 4th, for The Northumberland Fusiliers. As a consequence, the 3rd (Militia) Battalion was to be renumbered as the 5th (Militia) Battalion. The battalion, as part of the Malta Garrison, were guarding Boer Prisoners of War until 27 June 1901, when they embarked on the SS *Dilwara,* landing at Southampton on 7 July. Arriving at Alnwick around 8 a.m. on Monday 8 July, they marched through enthusiastic crowds to Alnwick Castle, where they were given breakfast in the Guest Hall. Later they were marched back to the Militia Barracks in Bondgate Without, where they handed in their uniforms and equipment, and were issued with a tweed suit and part of their bounty for service in Malta. They then travelled by special trains to their homes. A large crowd had assembled at the Central Station to welcome 440 men from Newcastle and the immediate district, who arrived shortly after 2 p.m.

A visit to Alnwick Castle by King Edward VII and Queen Alexandra, during the 1908 training of the battalion, saw the troops actively involved in the ceremonies that followed. On 10 July the streets of Alnwick were lined by the battalion, from the railway station to the castle via Fenkle Street. A Guard of Honour under the command of Major R. Scott, with the band and the King's colour carried by Lieutenant Durand, was mounted in the Inner Bailey of the castle. The band of the battalion under the leadership of Sergeant Drummer Cordial DCM, played at the castle during dinner on the 10th and 11th. The royal guests left Alnwick on 12 July. As well the Militia Battalion, a mounted escort of the Northumberland Hussars under the command of Lieutenant L. Johnstone accompanied the royal party, and a Guard of Honour of the 1st Volunteer Battalion, The Northumberland Fusiliers commanded by Major George Reavell, was mounted at the Bondgate Tower on the arrival of the royal party.

It was not until the beginning of the twentieth century that Richard Haldane, the Liberal Government Secretary of State for War (1905–1912), began a series of fundamental changes, between 1905 and 1908, to Britain's military capability, which were to have a significant impact upon the nation's relationship with Europe, particularly France and Belgium, as well an effect on the militia. One of the most radical reforms was the abolition of the militia, as it had been known for centuries. Its military function was to undergo extensive revision. Worst of all in the eyes of the militia, it was to become known as the Special Reserve. A new role as a training battalion for reinforcements for the regular battalions of

Militia memorial in St Michael's church, Alnwick. (J. Winter)

the Northumberland Fusiliers was to be adopted. This had a drastic effect upon recruitment; and for the local upper and middle classes it would lose its elitist character. It would never again serve as an operational battalion. So 1908 can be seen as a watershed in the history of the old 'Constitutional Force'. The battalion assembled for the last time as militia on 6 July 1908 for twenty-seven days' training at Alnwick. On the morning of the 29th the battalion was paraded in review order and the colours were marched in slow time through the ranks, the band playing the Troop St George. After this, the battalion marched up Denwick Lane, through the town to the castle, where they were formed up in quarter column in the Inner Bailey. They then presented arms and the colours and were marched off and lodged within the castle by Lieutenant Waddilove and Second Lieutenant Anne.

The first annual training in their new role as a Special Service Battalion began with a change of location. It was to be held on the Rifle Range at Moorlaws, about three and a half miles outside Alnwick, an isolated but beautiful site – in good weather! The road back to camp was uphill all the way, not conducive to a heavy night out on the town. Training for the years from 1909 to 1914 was held at the same spot. By 1913 numbers were very low, more then likely due to the location and monotony of the camp site, and the lack of leisure facilities. In June 1914, the battalion assembled once again for training. Little did anyone know of the momentous events that were to engulf them, and the cataclysmic war that was to follow. The writer of the battalion notes in *St George's Gazette*, July 1914, realises the shortcomings of Moorlaws, and makes the point that:

> Perhaps from a recruiting point of view our numbers would increase if we went for our
> training to a less isolated camp. At present there is the idea of a recruiting march through
> the county, but nothing has been settled to date.

Unknown to the writer of the notes there was going to be a flood of recruits in the very near future.

The 3rd (SR) Battalion mobilised at Alnwick on 6 August 1914 and proceeded to Newcastle to absorb its army reservists. Several companies moved out on detachment, guarding strategic locations in and around Newcastle. Headquarters and Recruit Companies were quartered in Canning Street Schools. The outlying detachments were called in, as they were relieved by units from the National Reserve. On Wednesday 23 September, Headquarters and 'B', 'C', 'D' and 'G' Companies, fully equipped and ready for service, moved to Scott's House Camp, West Boldon, County Durham, leaving four companies at Canning Street to train recruits. By this time over 500 men and 23 officers had been sent to join the 1st Battalion, Northumberland Fusiliers, in France. The strength of the battalion on 23 September 1914 was 2,011, all ranks. Two more companies, 'A' and 'E', moved into Scott's House Camp on 3 October.

The Corps of Drums of the 3rd (SR) Battalion NF at Scott's House, West Bolden, Co. Durham, c.1915.

During this period drafts were being sent to France, and huts were being erected in East Boldon to house the Service Companies. The first officer of the battalion to be wounded was Lieutenant Waddlilove, who had only left Newcastle three weeks previously. Over 200 wounded and invalids had been posted back to the battalion from France. The Service Companies moved into the new huts at East Boldon on 9 November and the Recruit Companies were relocated at Whitley Bay until new huts at Scott's House were ready. The camp there was by now a quagmire.

A permanent cadre of officers and senior ranks were employed on the instructing staff. There was a constant turnover of personnel. Drafts were sent overseas on a regular basis while new recruits were being trained. By 31 March 1915, the battalion had sent out 2,564 soldiers and 30 officers in drafts to the 1st and 2nd Battalions, Northumberland Fusiliers, in the front line. The permanent staff were to remain in County Durham for the remainder of the war. On Monday 3 March 1919 the battalion left East Boldon, after four years, for No. 13 Camp, Durrington, Salisbury Plain. In July the cadre of the 3rd (SR) Battalion returned to its peace-time station at Alnwick, and the remainder of the battalion was absorbed into the 1st Battalion. It seems fitting that the 3rd Battalion notes in *St George's Gazette*, 31 July 1919, should have the final word:

> The work done during the last five years by the battalion was at high pressure and on a large
> scale. Thankless work, largely unappreciated by the public and the authorities. But we know
> that it was for the regiment and that the regiment recognises its value. We filled up the 1st

Battalion with officers and other ranks in August 1914, and sent out the first reinforcements. The first Service Battalions to be formed, the 8th and 9th were formed largely from our personnel, which went also to form the first Garrison and Labour Battalions. All through the war we kept all the Line, Service, and Garrison Battalions alive with officers and other ranks and we regarded ourselves as the repository of the old traditions of the regiment. Five thousand offices and upwards of 23,000 other ranks passed through our hands. Officers and men [were] trained and retrained by the battalion, recruits and old hands were to be found in every battalion of the regiment, [and] in every theatre of war. The first VC won for the regiment since the [Indian] Mutiny was won by a 3rd Battalion recruit, Lance Corporal Bryan, and two other VCs were won by officers who had passed through the battalion. The battalion has been embodied in every war in which the country has been engaged since the time of Marlborough and we like to think that in this last and greatest of all wars our record has not been unworthy.

Thus ended the most important, if not the longest, embodiment of the battalion in its long history.

List of Embodiments:

The Seven Years' War: 25 February 1760 to December 1762, two years and ten months. CO Colonel Sir Edward Blackett, Bart.

The American War of Independence: 13 April 1778 to December 1782, four years and eight months. CO Colonel Lord Algernon Percy.

French Revolutionary War: January 1793 to 22 April 1802, nine years and five months. COs Colonel Lord Algernon Percy and Colonel John Reed. Owing to the over establishment of the battalion, Supplemental Battalion was formed – 2nd Northumberland Militia commanded by Colonel C.W. Bigge of Benton. During this period 373 men were drafted to the armies overseas.

French Napoleonic Wars: On termination of the Peace of Amiens in April 1803, up to 24 June 1814, eleven years and two months. COs Colonel John Reed, Lieutenant Colonel J.B. Coulson, Colonel Lord Lovaine. 1,159 NCOs and men were drafted to the line battalions, the Navy and Royal Marines during this embodiment.

Crimean War: 9 January 1855 to 20 June 1856, one year and five months. CO the Earl of Beverly. 395 men were drafted abroad at this time.

South Africa: 12 December to 12 July 1901, one year and seven months. CO Lord Algernon Percy ADC. Eighteen officers and 193 men went to the line battalions.

The First World War: 4 August 1914 to 12 July 1919, COs Colonel R.F. Roundel and Major C.P. Hawkes. 5,000 officers and 23,000 other ranks were drafted overseas in this period of embodiment.

INFORMATION FOR INTENDING RECRUITS.

The following information as to pay, bounty, &c., is for men wishing to join the 5th Battalion Northumberland Fusiliers :—

Men, who think they would like the life of a soldier, should first try it by joining the Militia. The advantage of this is, that if they do not like the life, it costs only £1 to purchase their discharge, whereas it costs £10 at least to purchase from the Regulars within the first three months, and considerably more afterwards. The life is practically the same, except that the Militia, being only out for one month, work at rather higher pressure. It is easy for a Militiaman to transfer to the Regular Army at any time.

Working men, who are living in towns, can get a month in the country as a change by joining the Militia. As they are fed and clothed, and draw over 50/- for the month, this is as cheap a way of getting a month in the country as could be found.

Every endeavour is made that the food supplied is ample and wholesome. Here is a diet return of one Company for a week, which gives a good idea as to how we feed you :—

5th BATTALION NORTHUMBERLAND FUSILIERS.

Diet Return at Malta for Week ending 15th June, 1901.

DAYS.	BREAKFAST.	DINNER.	TEA.
SUNDAY.	Coffee. Bread and Butter.	Plain Stew, Potatoes.	Tea, Bread, Butter, Cucumber and Lettuce.
MONDAY.	Coffee, Bread and Butter.	Celery Stew, Potatoes.	Tea, Bread, Butter, Cucumber and Lettuce.
TUESDAY.	Coffee, Bread, Butter and Bacon.	Roast Meat, Cabbage, Potatoes, Plum Pudding.	Tea, Bread, Butter, Cucumber and Lettuce.
WEDNESDAY.	Coffee, Bread and Butter	Sea Pie. Potatoes.	Tea, Bread, Butter, Cucumber and Lettuce.
THURSDAY.	Coffee, Bread and Butter.	Meat Pie, Cabbage and Potatoes.	Tea, Bread, Butter, Cucumber and Lettuce.
FRIDAY.	Coffee, Bread and Butter.	Plain Stew, Potatoes.	Tea, Bread, Butter, Cucumber and Lettuce.
SATURDAY.	Coffee, Bread, Butter and Bacon	Roast Meat, Cabbage and Potatoes, Plum Pudding.	Tea, Bread, Butter, Cucumber and Lettuce.

The top extract gives brief details of entry into the Militia. The bottom extract is obviously a menu for the soldiers of the battalion. The officers would have had a much more varied and richer diet. Source: Short History, 5th Battalion, Northumberland Fusiliers.

Extract from A Short History of the 5th Battalion NF *by Major G.F.T. Leather, 1902.*

The Special Reserve Battalion was never reformed. Along with the rest of the former militia, it was placed in suspended animation but was not formally disbanded until 1953. However, due to the threat in May 1939, parliament introduced a limited form of conscription through the passing of a Bill requiring every man on reaching the age of twenty to register for two years' compulsory service. It became known as the 'Militia Scheme'. On 2 September 1939, The National Service (Armed Forces) Bill, was introduced in parliament, under which all able-bodied men between the ages of eighteen and forty-one became liable for service 'for the duration of hostilities'. Conscription was to last until 1960.

THE NORTHUMBERLAND ARTILLERY MILITIA

This unit of the militia was first raised in July 1854. It was one of the smallest Artillery Corps to be raised at that time, with an establishment of 161, all ranks, including permanent staff. The headquarters of the corps was originally established at Tynemouth, but in December 1854 they were moved to Newcastle-upon-Tyne. The function of the corps was to act as a coastal defence artillery unit. Unfortunately their main claim to fame seems to have been a riot in North Shields. The *Newcastle Courant*, 18 May 1860, contains a report of the event. It seems that two gunners, Privates White and McKenna, were found drunk and causing a disturbance in Liddel Street on Monday 14 May. They were told by the police to go back to their barracks. McKenna struck PC McClaren in the face. With the assistance of a river policeman, he was arrested. Another policeman, PC Batey, seeing that White was going to assist McKenna, took hold of him. White managed to get away and, running along the street, met PC Cockburn, who he struck in the face.

The next day, Tuesday 15th, they were fined £2, or one month's imprisonment. On Tuesday night about thirty militiamen wandered the streets, attacking any they came across with sticks and, a favourite soldier's weapon, their belts. PC Cockburn was on New Quay when he saw a gang of militiamen coming towards him, so he took refuge on a ship tied up at quay. PC Hunter was beaten up in Clive Street. PC Shirley was very badly beaten, and was taken by some civilians into Mr Walker's butchers shop in Bedford Street. The militiamen forced the door off its hinges and tore the clothes off PC Shirley. PC Thompson was knocked down opposite the Catholic church and was severely injured. The report states that, 'This officer lies in a precarious state.' After this incident, they dispersed. The commanding officer, Colonel Clementson, sent out a piquet of fifty men under the command of Captain McBay to capture the rioters. Hundreds of people congregated on the streets to see if the piquet made any arrests.

Eleven militiamen were eventually turned over to the magistrates. William Warburton, John Dickinson, Joseph Mill, John Gallagher, Patrick Atkinson, Michael Kennedy, John Anderson, John Randells, William Morgan, Joseph Spence, Lionel Bolton, and a woman, Isabella Woods, were charged with creating a riot and violently assaulting Police Constables Hunter, Shirley and Thompson, on Tuesday evening. The case was adjourned due to the policemen not being able to appear.

The men were remanded to Morpeth Jail, and Isabella Wood to the House of Correction. That night, extra police from Northumberland Constabulary and a strong piquet from the militia patrolled the streets for several hours. It is interesting to note that the two men who started the trouble were not among those arrested as rioters. General Sir John Pennyfather, Officer Commanding Northern District, inspected the Artillery Militia at Tynemouth on the afternoon of Monday 21 May. In the absence of the mayor of Tynemouth, Sir John sent for Mr A.B. Stevenson, one of the Tynemouth Borough magistrates, and expressed his personal regret, as head of the military in the district, about what had occurred between the militia and the police, stating that, 'The military authorities would do all they could to restore good feeling'. He also said that Lieutenant Colonel Clementson had applied to have the regiment moved from Tynemouth.

But the trouble was not over. Another militiaman, Thomas Bates, was charged with beating a young woman for giving evidence against his comrades at the late trial. The magistrates sentenced him to one month's hard labour in the House of Correction. The behaviour of the militiamen so disgusted the townspeople that they requested that they be removed from the Tynemouth area. Obviously the military authorities moved swiftly to pacify fears. The *Newcastle Courant*, Friday 8 June, reported: 'On Wednesday morning [6th] the Northumberland Artillery Militia left Tynemouth Castle for Liverpool, en-route to their new quarters on Spike Island, Cork, Ireland.' Their comrades were left behind to face the consequences of their riotous behaviour. Under the headline 'The Militia Outrage at Tynemouth', the *Newcastle Courant*, Friday 6 July, informed its readers that:

> At the Northumberland Quarter Sessions held at Hexham, on Thursday 5 July, the following: William Warburton, (22), John Dickinson (21), Joseph Mills (20), John Anderson (18), John Gallagher (20), William Morgan (21), Lionel Bolton (20), soldiers of the Northumberland Artillery Militia, and Isabella Wood (20) single woman, were severally charged with rioting at South Shields on 15 May 1860.

It would appear that the charges against Patrick Atkinson, Michael Kennedy, John Randells and Joseph Spence had not been pursued. The *Newcastle Journal*, of Saturday 7 July 1860 states:

there was the unusual number of 28 prisoners for trial, but the only one of importance was that of the men belonging to the Northumberland Artillery Militia and the woman charged with riot at Shields, and the attack on the police.

At their trial, Lionel Bolton was found not guilty, and the rest, including Isabella Wood, were given one months hard labour to be served in Morpeth Jail.

This event may have led to the headquarters of the Militia Artillery eventually being transferred to Ravensdowne Barracks, Berwick-upon-Tweed, in September 1861. On the other hand, it could have been that the barracks were empty at that time and it may have seemed an ideal opportunity to have them occupied. The *Berwick Advertiser*, 5 February 1859, noted:

> Some members of our community, alas, understanding that the government do not mean again to occupy with troops the barracks in this town, have commenced helping themselves to the materials with they are composed. On Tuesday [1 February] we understand, it was discovered that about four hundredweights [448 lbs.] [203.63 Kilos] of lead had been stripped from the roof and carried off.

Captain Way was serving in the Regimental Depot of the Fifth (Northumberland) Fusiliers in the barracks, when he first met the Artillery Militia in 1879. In his diary, published in the *St George's Gazette*, July 1942, he wrote:

> The militia trained at Dunbar, Scotland, this year, and we often used to go to dine with them. The men were a very fine lot, great, strong, sturdy Northumbrians; there were often very funny stories about them. One morning a gunner appeared on parade and was spotted by his officer as not having any boots on; he said he had sold them, and hoping to escape detection, he had blacked his feet.

The unit was mobilised for full-time service from 4 April 1859 to 2 March 1861 – it was during this embodiment that the riot took place – again from 7 May 1900 to 11 October 1900, due to the South African War. In 1874 the establishment of the corps had been increased to 450 men in five batteries. This was increased again in 1882 by a further battery, and the corps assumed the title 3rd Brigade, Northern Division, Royal Artillery, which was changed again in 1889 to the Northumberland Artillery (Western Division) Royal Artillery. The unit was renamed as The Northumberland Royal Garrison Artillery (Militia) in 1902, which it retained until transfer to the Royal Field Artillery (Special Reserve) in 1908. It was finally disbanded in 1909, another victim of the Haldane reforms of 1908.

TWO

THE REVOLUTIONARY AND NAPOLEONIC WARS 1793–1815

Of a' the many bonny corps,
Which now our country nigh fill,
Where can ye shew me sic a corps,
As the bonny Wallsend Rifles,
The canny Wallsend Rifles,
Where can ye shew me sic a corps,
As the bonny Wallsend Rifles.

John Bell, Newcastle, 1812.

Initially, the French Revolution of 1798 was not viewed as a threat to the British Isles. It was welcomed by many in political circles, as well as by dissenters and radicals, as an end to monarchical absolutism in France. Young poets of the period, such as Samuel Taylor Coleridge and William Wordsworth, expressed their delight and praise for the revolution through verse. There was a proliferation of radical reform clubs and societies proposing social and political argument and change.

But some saw the situation in a different light. Edmund Burke, a Whig politician, wrote his *Reflections on the French Revolution* (1790), a publication which influenced opposition to the revolution all over Europe. Becoming alarmed by the reaction to Thomas Paine's *The Rights of Man* (1792) and its support for individualist democratic reform, the government of the day, under Prime Minister William Pitt (1783–1801), initiated a policy of political repression against the fledgling democratic associations. The European monarchs were appalled and alarmed by the activities of the French revolutionaries, who set out to spread their version of democracy by a crusade of a 'nation in arms'. British government warnings to France convinced some revolutionaries that war would lead to revolution in Britain. Consequently, France declared war against Britain on 1 February 1793.

This led William Pitt to send a circular to the Lords Lieutenant of counties on the need for volunteers to repel an invasion:

Plan of Augmentation, 17 March 1794

Companies of infantry for manning batteries on the coast each to consist of : - One captain, 2 lieutenants, 3 sergeants, 2 corporals, 60 private men, - least - one third to be armed with firelocks, the others to have pikes 8 feet long. Officers to be recommended by Lords Lieutenant, but commissions come from the King. To assemble two days each week to practise. Officers to be allowed pay. NCOs and men 1s [5p] a day for exercise. Uniforms supplied by the government were to be red for infantry, artillery blue, rifles green with black belts. To be supplied once every three years at a cost of: Sergeants £3 3s 9d, [£3.19]; Corporals £1 12s 0d, [£1.60]; Drummers £2 3s [£2.15]; Privates £1 10s 0d [£1.50]. Not to be removed more then five miles from home, unless ordered by His Majesty on appearance of invasion; then not to moved out of the county.

Almost immediately the government received offers of voluntary service from all over the British Isles, nowhere more enthusiastically than in the area between the Rivers Tyne and Tweed. There was reason to fear that local forces in the maritime counties might be called out at any time so the supply of arms was geared to those counties. The defence of Newcastle-upon-Tyne was recommended for special attention (see *County Lieutenancies and the Army 1803–1814*). In Newcastle, two units of volunteer infantry were formed. The Revd J.C. Bruce, in his *Handbook to Newcastle upon Tyne 1863*, states:

The [Loyal] Newcastle Volunteer Infantry, force of between 300 and 400 strong, was chiefly recruited from the aristocratic class of the inhabitants. Their uniforms [red with green facings] being somewhat gay, they received the by-name of 'The Tinsel Dons'. They were under the command of Colonel Thomas Clennel. The [Loyal] Newcastle Associated Infantry, consisting for the most part of men of the middle and lower class, formed a regiment of from 800 to 1,000 strong. It was commanded by Sir Matthew White Ridley, the father of the present baronet.

The government originally wanted to use the volunteers as additions to the militia, but this was not a popular move. The average private saw himself as superior to the militiamen, and the volunteer officers were usually wealthy gentlemen of some standing and influence in their community, who were prepared to make considerable sacrifices of time, effort and money, for what they viewed as their patriotic duty. They did not want to be seen to be just making up the numbers of a socially inferior militia. Perhaps the fact that volunteers were exempted from the militia ballot was an added incentive. As a result, on 28 March 1794, the government passed an amendment to the Volunteer Act of 1782. (34 George III c.16): 'An Act for augmenting the Militia and raising Volunteer Companies and additional Volunteer privates.' This was followed on 12 April 1794 by the Volunteer Act 1794, (34 Geo. III. c. 31): 'An Act for Encouraging and Disciplining such Corps or Companies of Men as shall voluntarily enrol themselves for the defence of their Counties, Towns, or Coasts, or for the general defences of the Kingdom, during the present war.'

There are numerous references to the various corps of volunteers from the Tyne to the Tweed, in the newspapers of the period, which can be found in Newcastle Central Library. A song – *The Newcastle Volunteers* – appears in the *Newcastle Courant*, 18 July 1795, from which the following extract is taken:

> Thus finithed , Mars fpoke, 'Great Jove with your leave,
> Some youths in Newcastle I have,
> Their laws to defend-let me arms to them give,
> For their country all dangers they'll brave,'
> Cry'd Jove, 'Be it so, intruft it to them,'
> And the Gods with three heavenly cheers,
> Confented, while Jove did give them the name,
> Of the NEWCASTLE LOY'L VOLUNTEERS.

This corps was composed of those who were affluent enough to be able to purchase their own uniforms, arms and equipment, and serve without pay. On the other hand, the members of the Newcastle Armed Association were supplied by the government with their uniforms (red with blue facings), weapons and equipment. In this unit there were also riflemen whose uniform was green with green facings, black lace and black trousers. As well as training for the defence of Newcastle and the surrounding area, the volunteers were also involved in the social and cultural life of the town. On Thursday 25 February 1808, a report in the *Newcastle Courant* tells us that:

> The theatre here was uncommonly crowded, the play being under the patronage of Lieutenant Colonel Ridley and the Newcastle Associated Volunteer Infantry. When the curtain drew up after the play, the initials of the corps appeared in large illuminated letters through two arches of evergreens, and had a brilliant effect.

It was not only in Newcastle that volunteers came forward. In towns and villages throughout Northumberland, committees were formed, intent upon raising bodies of local volunteers to defend their own locations if the need arose. The market towns of Hexham, Morpeth, Alnwick, Rothbury, Wooler, Berwick-upon-Tweed, and the rural villages, hamlets and estates of Northumberland, raised numerous armed units. Examples of these were the Royal Cheviot Legion, Infantry and Cavalry, raised in 1798 from the inhabitants of Wooler and the surrounding district, and the Coquetdale Rangers, raised in 1799.

A muster roll in Northumberland Record Office dated 20 September 1803, of the Royal Cheviot Legion Infantry and Cavalry, commanded by Colonel Horace St Paul, of Ewart House, Doddington, shows his thirty infantry officers living as far apart as Felton in the south of the county, and Flodden in the north; to Bamburgh in the east and Wooler in the west. Of the infantry of other ranks shown on the roll, 140 came from Wooler, two from Chillingham, eleven from Chatton, three from Doddington and two from Kirknewton. Among the Wooler men were trades of nailor, matchmaker, shoemaker, clogger, barber, innkeeper, stocking-maker, weaver, baker, tailor, hatter, thatcher, butcher, cooper, flax-dresser and whitesmith. These diverse occupations reflect the self-sufficiency of the small, rural market towns and villages in the period before the development of the road and rail system that created easier access to the isolated areas of north Northumberland.

The seven officers and eighty-four troopers of the Royal Cheviot Legion Cavalry were scattered over a very wide area. Among then were eighteen from Rothbury, twenty-three from Whittingham, three from Alnham, nine from Wooler, four from Chillingham and six from Eglingham. It is very likely that the bulk of the members would have been agricultural workers who had access to horses. Some of the places of residence listed may not exist today – for instance, the homes of James Robson of Half Crown Hall; John Donkin of Plainfield; William Walby of Dewshill; Caleb Hastings of Thrunton Mill; John Crozier of Newton Mill; Thomas Redy of Hethpool Mill; and William McCreath of Learmouth Mill. Frequent changes of address would seem to indicate there may have been a good deal of movement among the men, perhaps due to the annual hiring of agricultural workers in Northumberland.

Regiments of cavalry seemed to have been popular in north Northumberland. As well as the Cheviot Legion, there was the Coquetdale Troop of Volunteer Cavalry. A muster roll dated November 1896 (NRO), shows fifty-five officers and men commanded by Captain Thomas Selby of Biddlestone, an ancient Northumberland family which appears in the rolls of the Northumberland Militia and the Northumberland Hussars in later years. The other officers were Lieutenant John Mills of Whittingham and Cornet William Wilson of Rothbury. Though raised in 1799, the earliest date of enrolment on the existing muster rolls is 22 November 1805. They had, however, gone on

Coquetdale Volunteer Cavalry, Tarleton helmet. Badge Prince of Wales feather and motto – 'Ich Dien'. Leopard skin turban (N. Farrier).

permanent duty for three weeks at Berwick with the North Durham Yeomanry (*Newcastle Courant*, Saturday 21 July). The Coquetdales must have looked quite splendid when parading in uniform. It consisted of a brass helmet with black horsehair plume, scarlet tunic, white breeches and a large scarlet cloak.

David Dippie Dixon writes in his book, *Whittingham Vale* (Newcastle, 1895), of the night when both the Coquetdale Rangers and the Cheviot Legion turned out for the 'False Alarm' on Tuesday 31 January 1804. A French invasion was thought imminent when the beacons were lit, and both units galloped from their homes, which were scattered all over Coquetdale and Glendale, to their predetermined rallying point in Glanton. By daybreak there was a full muster of the Cheviot Legion, 'who, for its loyalty and despatch, henceforth received the name of the Royal Cheviot Legion.' The Coquetdale Rangers from Glendale had much further to ride. Captain Thomas Selby was in Edinburgh, and a messenger was sent to seek him, 'it is said that the gallant Captain never recovered from the effects of his long and rapid ride from Edinburgh to Glanton.' When authentic news was received that the French had not landed, 'the Troopers spent the remainder of the day at Glanton in that social and jovial manner for which our Yeoman ancestors were so famous.' David Dippie Dixon was probably suggesting that they were drunk before they returned to their homes!

A letter dated 1 August 1805, from Lieutenant Colonel Charles Rawdon, Inspecting Field Officer, to Colonel Horace St Paul, quoted in Colonel J.G. Hicks' *The Volunteers of a Hundred Years Ago* (Newcastle, 1904), gives an insight into the workings of the Home Defence Force:

> Sir, Agreeably to instructions this day received, I have the honour to inform you of the route fixed on for the march of the Royal Cheviot Legion towards Stilton in case of an alarm, and of their quarters, of field equipment, with the place of depot.
>
> Royal Cheviot. – 697 establishment. four-fifths, 588, expected to march.
> 19 tents; 112 kettles.
> Depot, Alnwick. Place of assembly, Alnwick.
> 1st day's march, Newcastle, 36 miles.
> 2nd day's march, Darlington, 31 miles.
> 3rd day's march, Northallerton, 16 miles.
> Officers not included; sergeants and corporals and drummers are.

The Cheviot Legion had obviously volunteered to serve outside the county. There was some hard marching to come.

An item in the *Newcastle Courant*, 26 September 1807, mentions that Thomas Davidson, of Alwinton, a trumpeter who had deserted from Captain Selby's Troop of the Coquetdale Rangers, was being sent back to Biddlestone, the headquarters of the troop, with an escort from the Newcastle Loyal Volunteers. The escort, no doubt, would not have been too pleased about the march in front of them. The Rangers were still in existence in 1821, by this time 183 strong, and commanded by Captain John Collingwood Tarlaton.

A short-lived corps was the Loyal Glendale Rangers, which in 1801 consisted of Captain George Adam Askew and thirty-four effectives. This small unit had an impressive standard which is described by Colonel Hicks:

> White, in the centre on a large red ground is 'Loyal Glendale Rangers' surrounded by a crown of evergreen. In the first and fourth corners a white horse rampant; second and third corners, the initials L.G.R. on a red ground. On the reverse, 'Pro Rege et Patria' in the centre. Size 33 inches by 20 inches with forked end.

At the time Hicks wrote this description, the standard was in the possession of Watson Askew Robertson, of Pallinsburn, nephew of Captain Askew. This corps did not appear in the 1803 Army List. In 1803, however, there was a Glendale Volunteer Cavalry commanded by Major Lord Ossulston, with two officers and fifty-two effectives, and the Glendale Volunteer Infantry also commanded by

Tunic. Scarlet with green facings and gilt buttons.
(N. Farrier)

Major Lord Ossulston with three officers and sixty-two effectives in 1804; by 1806 this number had risen to 121.

By far the largest, best-recruited and best-equipped in Northumberland and Tyneside were the Percy Tenantry Volunteers, raised and entirely funded, apart from government-issued weapons, by Hugh Percy (1786–1817), the second Duke of Northumberland. This regiment was not raised without some controversy. The *Alnwick Journal*, 16 April 1860, contains an article concerning the furore aroused by the attempts of some townspeople of Alnwick to form an 'Armed Association'. This resulted in a declaration from the chairman of the committee, stating that the Duke of Northumberland showed:

A marked opposition to it; but treated it contemptuously; deeming it a great presumption to embark in the measure without his concurrence; notifying all his dependants, or those whom he conceived as such, his expectation that none of them would engage in the same, seemingly arrogating to himself, the sole ability and right to determine on its expediency; and finally, ordering all those tradesmen to be deprived of his custom, and discharging from his employment, who in following the dictates of their own judgements, and honestly adhering to their country's cause, had enrolled themselves in the said Association.

The cause of the above declaration was a letter from the Duke of Northumberland to the Honourable Mr Dormer and Robert Forster Esq., dated 3 March 1797:

This idea is really too ridiculous, and I cannot say that I think it very polite in these gentlemen, to take a step of this kind under my very nose, without so much as giving themselves the trouble to inform me of their intentions; and I trust that no tenant or tradesman whom I employ will join them without first knowing my sentiments on the subject. Having as much property as these gentlemen who wish to appear so active, and being naturally inclined from my profession to defend that property as well as them, my tenants and dependants may be assured, that if I foresaw any real danger, I should not myself fail to call upon them to assist me in the defence of everything that is dear to man; and I trust from their relative situations with regard to me, as well as from the military knowledge I ought to possess after forty years service, that they will on such occasion be more willing to follow me, their landlord, than those gentlemen who conceive that creating an alarm in the county, and putting on a red coat and cockade, entitles them to the confidence due to a commander. I therefore flatter myself that my tenants and other dependants will keep themselves disengaged 'till I call upon them, and they may depend upon it that NOBODY WILL BE MORE READY TO LEAD THEM ON, OR GO FURTHER TO DEFEND THEIR PROPERTY, AND THE CONSTITUTION OF THIS COUNTRY, AGAINST ALL ITS ENEMIES, THAN I WILL IF OCCASION SHOULD REQUIRE IT.

King's colour (George III) of the Percy Tenantry and the Guidon of the Percy Tenantry Cavalry, c.1806. (Courtesy of Northumberland Estates)

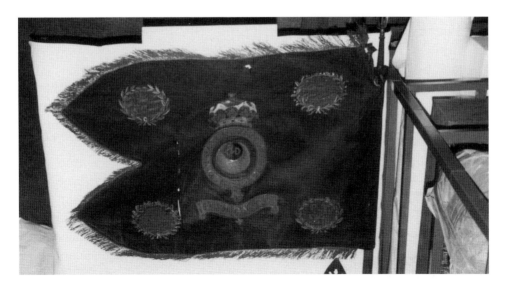

Guidon of Percy Tenantry Cavalry. (J. Winter)

This was almost a feudal response; the message to the employees and tenants of his estate, and the shopkeepers and other small businesses in Alnwick and the surrounding district, was quite clear, essentially amounting to, 'You serve in my regiment or you are in trouble'. So the reality was that it amounted to a form of volunteering by coercion.

The Armed Association of the Percy Tenantry Infantry was raised on the duke's extensive estates in Northumberland and Tyneside. The southern division, enrolled on 11 May 1798, commanded by Christopher Blackett as Major Commandant, consisted of four companies and, by a return dated 7 February 1799, numbered 275 men. The northern division, commanded by Major John Watson, consisted of eight companies. A muster roll of the Percy Tenantry Volunteer Cavalry enrolled on 11 May 1798, shows by a return dated 7 February 1799:

1st Troop: Captain Anthony Lambert	47
2nd Troop: Captain William Hay	64
3rd Troop: Captain John Pratt	36
4th Troop: Captain Henry Coward	53
5th Troop: Captain Charles Newton	52
TOTAL	252

In August 1806, the cavalry were on permanent duty for ten days, and received new clothing and helmets. The Duchess of Northumberland presented the unit with new standards, one of which still exists within the castle collections. Hugh,

Earl Percy, the eldest son, was appointed to the command of the whole regiment on 30 July 1803. The first return after that date shows six troops of cavalry at Alnwick, Lesbury, Newham, Newburn, Prudhoe and Tynemouth, with a strength of 304 men. There were seventeen companies of infantry: Alnwick, Chatton, Guyzance and Thirston, Lesbury, Newham, Rothbury, Shillbottle, Warkworth, Barrasford (two), Lemington, Newburn (two), Prudhoe (two), and Tynemouth, strength 1,195, total enrolled 1,500.

A new arm was added to the duke's private army in January 1805, when the Percy Tenantry Volunteer Artillery Company, attached to the cavalry, was enrolled under the command of Captain John Toppin, 12 February 1805, who had resigned his command of the Corbridge Volunteers. The establishment of the Percy Artillery was twenty-six, which remained unaltered. This company was issued with two brass three-pounders, and the necessary equipment and harness of Horse Artillery by the government. Among those who joined the artillery was Henry Kirk, whose father had served as a sergeant in the Light Company of the 5th Foot (later The Royal Northumberland Fusiliers) during the American War of Independence, under the command of Hugh, Earl Percy (later 2nd Duke of Northumberland), and then employed as a porter in the Barbican of the castle. He is buried in St Michael's churchyard, in Alnwick. The young Kirk's maternal grandfather, Thomas Bamborough, also enlisted but lost a leg during gun drill and was given a pension of 7s [35p] per week by the duke.

The *Newcastle Courant*, 4 November 1809, describes an impressive ceremony which was enacted in the small market town of Alnwick, on 25 October, to celebrate the fiftieth year of George III's reign, and gives us a word picture of one event in the activities of Hugh Percy's Tenantry Volunteers:

> … the Jubilee was celebrated at Alnwick with such spirit and loyalty. The morning was ushered in by the ringing of bells, and the reveille by the drums of the Northumberland regiment of local militia, and by the bugles of the Percy Tenantry Volunteers, who were stationed on the turrets over the great gates of the castle, from the saluting battery of which a gun was fired at sunrise, and the flag hoisted. Before noon the brigade of artillery, the detachment of 17 rifle wall-pieces, three troops of cavalry (with the ancient standards of the family) and nine companies of riflemen, being the northern half of the corps of the Percy Tenantry, marched into Alnwick Castle, where refreshments were provided for them; after which they took post on the battlement towers, and top of the castle … Immediately after divine service, the salute commenced with seven guns from the artillery, which was followed by all the wall pieces, and *feu de joie* from the cavalry, drawn up under the castle, which was succeeded by three cheers, and then a flourish from the bugles in the flag tower. This was twice repeated, completing the royal salute of 21 guns; after which the troops and companies returned immediately to their several places of muster, where dinners were provided for them. The officers of the corps on

duty at Alnwick, dined with their colonel, the Earl Percy, at the castle, where they were most elegantly and hospitably entertained, and 'God save the King' was sung in full chorus, after his majesty's health was drunk. The fineness of the weather added much to the festivity of the day, and induced a great number of ladies to go into the ground, opposite the castle, where the firing could be seen with the greatest effect. At the town hall, in the evening, there was a ball most fashionably and numerously attended by all the families of the neighbourhood ... The other half of the corps upon Tyneside, also fired a *feu de joie,* on Throckly Fell, after which the officers dined together in Newcastle, and the men in their respective places of muster. Jubilee medals, in honour of the day, were delivered to all the officers and serjeants of this corps, which consists of above 1,500 men paid by His Grace the Duke of Northumberland.

After disbanding the Percy Tenantry in 1814, the artillery continued to keep up their drills, though vacancies do not seem to have been filled. Government equipment was returned to ordnance and the duke provided six-pounder guns with which they trained. An ex-Royal Artillery man, John Thompson, was appointed as armourer and gunner to the corps. In 1840, William Williams was appointed as armourer and gunner to the corps, and in 1848 was appointed as Keeper in Abbey Lodge. A report appeared in the *Newcastle Courant,* 28 November 1845:

On Tuesday the 18th inst., the Duke of Northumberland's Household Artillery, under the command of Mr Williams, late gunner 8th Battalion, Royal Artillery, were reviewed on the castle green, Alnwick, by Captain Bloomfield, of the Royal Horse Artillery, Newcastle. The captain was accompanied by several gentlemen who were on a visit to the castle. The gunners went through their various exercises with great rapidity of movement; and Captain Bloomfield expressed his approbation of their efficiency and deportment. The Duke of Northumberland gave the gunners a supper on Tuesday last, Mr James Bowmaker in the chair; the supper was provided by Mr William Dunn of the *Nag's Head Inn.*

It had become, in effect, an exclusive militaristic social club with the kudos of being the duke's personal artillery corps. It was eventually responsible for the raising of the new corps of Percy Artillery Volunteers in 1859.

Being a Royal Garrison, perhaps the town most fought-over by the English and the Scots, as well as its status as a port making it a prime target for attack or invasion, it is not surprising that Berwick was among the first to raise bodies of volunteers. The first recorded unit in the town was raised on 23 May 1794, under Major Commandant Thomas Hall. In 1797 the corps, entitled the Loyal Berwick Volunteers, was increased to four companies, with Major Hall being promoted to Lieutenant Colonel. Following the Armed Association Act of 1798, the Berwick Gentlemen Independent Volunteers were enrolled on 31 May 1798, to serve without pay, with Major Burnett Grieve, who had been the Junior Cornet of the

Loyal Berwicks in 1794, in command. Their total strength in 1801 was eighty-nine. The town also boasted the Berwick Artillery Volunteers, which first appears in the Lieutenancy Muster Rolls on 13 December 1804, with a strength of three officers, twelve NCOs, seventy-four gunners, one drummer (David Learmouth), and one drill sergeant, commanded by Captain John Henderson. They last appear in the rolls on 10 August 1813, with a strength of seventy-two, commanded by Captain George Burns from 1807, with William Scoular as Sergeant Major. Under the above Act of 1798, Lords Lieutenant were empowered to make returns of:

> Men residing in each place between the ages of fifteen and sixty, distinguishing those incapable through infirmity, and those already serving in Volunteer corps, and stating which of them are willing to engage themselves to be armed, arrayed, trained and exercised for the defence of the kingdom, and which of them are willing to engage, in case of emergency, either gratuitously or for hire, as boatmen, drivers, and in various other capacities. Aliens and Quakers to be classed apart.

The Act was limited to continuance of the war with France. These Armed Associations were distinguished from the ordinary Volunteer corps in that their duties were purely local and their main function seems to have been to act as a guerrilla force, aiding the civil power during the evacuation of the civilian population in the event of invasion.

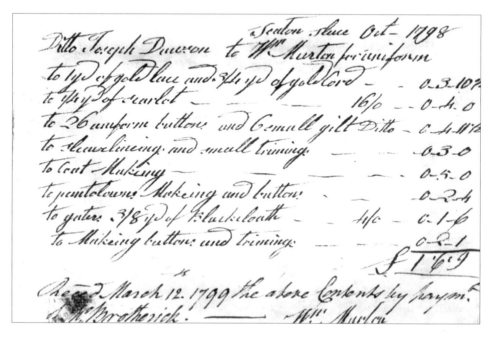

Receipt for purchase of uniform for 'Seaton Delaval Householders', 12 March 1799. (Northumberland Record Office)

Shoulder belt plate of the 'Seaton Delaval Householders', c.1800. (J. Winter)

Under the Armed Association Act, details of which can be found among the Delaval papers (NRO), was that of the people of Seaton Delaval. On 24 March 1794, Mr Jack Carr, estate agent at Ford Castle, sent a letter to Mr John Bryers of Seaton Lodge, Seaton Delaval, in which he wrote:

> In a little time I expect to hear an early example of a small community forming themselves into a corps of volunteers of your being appointed captain of a company to defend our coast, if so, and you should meet the French patriots in the field, be sure to immortalise the name of Captain Bryers by feats of valour, and drive the French dogs into the bosom of Neptune again'.

The earliest reference appertaining to the Seaton Delaval Associated Corps of Volunteer Infantry, are among the Delaval papers, which contains a note stating that they were enrolled between 24 May and 19 June 1798, and that Lord Delaval found the arms, accoutrements and ammunition; strength seventy-two. There is also a muster roll, undated, showing three companies: Grenadier Company, eighteen men over 5ft 8in tall; a Light Infantry Company, twenty-two men over 5ft 7in; and a Battalion Company, twenty men over 5ft 6in – sixty in all. According to a John Robinson, who compiled a short unpublished account of the Volunteers in 1891, Captain Bryers was 6ft in his stocking feet and weighed 18 stone 6 pounds – an imposing man. This was a little corps which was self-sufficient, receiving no financial support from the government, and could be used as a model on which to base the activities of most of the rural volunteer units throughout the country. They drilled and exercised at 6 p.m. on Tuesdays, fortnightly in the summer, and 3 p.m. on Tuesdays, once a month in the winter.

In accordance with the Act mentioned above, measures had been formulated for action in response to an invasion. A return of those to be evacuated from the Township of Seaton Delalval, and Parish of Earsdon, shows twenty-eight householders listed. There were forty-five infants, six infirm and seven aged; thirty-two carts were to be provided to convey them. Each householder was issued with a ticket showing the number of the cart allocated to them. The origins of the carts are listed below:

Name:	Carts:	Marked:
Lord Delaval	3	1-2-3
Robert Swan	5	4-5-6-7-8
William Huggup	3	9-10-11
William Swan	2	12-13
William Chicken	2	14-15
Joseph Oxley	2	16-17
Henry Ridlay & Co.	7	18-19-20-21-22-23-24
John Cairns	2	25-26
Jacob Wood	4	27-28-29-30
Henry Liddle	2	31-32

It is very likely that the Morpeth, Corbridge and Hexham Corps would have been raised and financed under the same conditions as the Seaton Delaval Volunteers. It was mainly the units raised and financed under patronage of one sort or another, that were able to serve without government financial support. Among them was the Morpeth Associated Volunteer Infantry raised on 6 July 1799, and commanded by Captain John Bell, with a strength of seventy-eight. In 1801 he was styled as Major Commandant, with a strength of 125. A certificate from John Bell specifies the conditions under which this corps was enrolled:

I, John Bell, as commanding officer of the Morpeth Associated Corps of Volunteer Infantry (serving without pay), do hereby certify (in pursuance of an Act 39 Geo. III.) that the conditions of service agreed to by the said Association are as follows: - That the said Association hath consented that every person enrolled shall find his own clothing and serve without pay, except when employed in actual service, and then to receive such allowances and assistance from government as is mentioned in a circular letter from the Hon. Henry Dundas, dated 6 April 1798. The said Association not to be compelled to serve at a further distance than ten miles from the Town of Morpeth. That the government is to find arms, ammunition, and accoutrements for the said Association, and that all and every person named in the annual muster roll have duly signified their consent to the above conditions of service by their signature to the said muster roll. Sunday afternoon at 6 o'clock is the day of exercise at Morpeth.

As a mark of respect to Admiral Collingwood, of Trafalgar fame, the corps paraded outside his residence in Morpeth (Oldgate) on one of his rare visits to his home. A reporter of the *Newcastle Advertiser*, 2 March 1799, wrote:

> The Morpeth Volunteers on Wednesday last, after leaving the ground where they had exercised, marched opposite to Admiral Collingwood's house, where they drew up, and on the Admiral's appearance immediately presented arms, when Captain Bell, in the name of his corps, in a very appropriate and elegant speech congratulated the Admiral on his late well-merited promotion, and at the same time presented the wishes of the corps that he might long live to wear the laurels he had so nobly and worthily gained, after which they gave him three cheers.

The corps does not appear in the army list of 1803.

The Corbridge Volunteer Corps of Infantry was enrolled in 1804 with a uniform of red with yellow facings and white breeches, under the command of Captain John Toppin, who has already been noted as resigning to take command of the Percy Tenantry Artillery. He was succeeded by Captain John Harbottle in 1805, and the strength at that time was seventy. Further up the Tyne Valley the Hexham Volunteer Infantry, eighty strong, had been formed in 1801 with Captain William Bell in command. By 1804 the numbers had increased to 140, with Major William Carr promoted over Captain Bell, who was still serving. Their uniform was also red with yellow facings. Another short-lived unit was the Wallington and Kirkharle Volunteer Troop of Cavalry, raised in 1799 with Captain John Trevelyan, Lieutenant William Loraine and forty-two troopers. This small cavalry troop also does not appear on the Army List for 1803.

The demise of the units which did not appear in the 1803 Army List would have been due to the general disbandment of these early corps of volunteers after the signing of the 'Peace of Amiens', which was proclaimed in Newcastle on 4 May 1802. The Newcastle Volunteers, The Armed Association, and the Gateshead Volunteers, mustered on the Sandhill at 12.00 p.m., and took part in the proceedings. They were met by the mayor, aldermen, Sheriff, and others, attended by General Murray and many other officers and gentlemen. The proclamation was read, ushered in by trumpets, the town sword was sheathed, the volunteers presented arms and the band played 'God Save the King'. The Newcastle Loyal Volunteers were disbanded on 15 June and they publicly deposited their colours at the Mansion House.

On 27 July the Newcastle Armed Association was also disbanded and they deposited their arms and standard at the Merchant's Hall in the Sandhill. It was to be a short-lived peace, and war was again declared with France on 18 May 1803. On that same day, the members of the Loyal Volunteers held a meeting convened by the mayor, Thomas Clennel, their former commanding officer, and they resolved to offer their services to the government. On 16 July the

Newcastle Advertiser published the following statement: 'His Majesty has been graciously pleased to accept, in the greatest approbation, the offer of services made by Sir W.M. Ridley, Bart., on behalf of the members of the late Armed Association'.

On the river Tyne the volunteers had obviously not been disbanded. The North Shields and Tynemouth Volunteer Infantry, raised in 1800 by Captain William Linskill, with 171 members had, by 1805, expanded to 332. By then, William Linskill had been promoted to Lieutenant Colonel. Sykes, in *Local Records* 1833, Vol.11, reports that the corps had:

> Entered upon permanent duty for one month. The guards of Clifford's Fort, Tynemouth Barracks, and the Spanish Battery were delivered up to them. The company in Clifford's Fort had not been in possession of it for more than four hours when Major Doyle of the Light Brigade from Sunderland, crossed the Tyne in a large flat-bottomed boat, with one company of the 61st Regiment, one company of Northumberland Militia, and one company of the Lanark Militia. The Major galloped up to the Fort gate and demanded entrance, but was answered by Colonel Linskill in the negative. The Colonel instantly made a signal for reinforcements, when another company of volunteers marched up the hill from Dockwray Square and commenced a sharp sham action on the Low Lights Bridge, while the men in the Fort made a sally, and the battle became general. Much skill and apparent courage were displayed on both sides, the contending parties at intervals charging [with] bayonets, and the engagement ended in a retreat of the assailants. During the contest a party of volunteers crossed the Tyne and struck the tents of the besieging party.

Further up the Tyne the Wallsend Volunteer Rifle Corps, commanded by John Buddle Jr, had 145 effectives in 1804. They were trained as Light Infantrymen and wore a green tunic with black facings, and black trousers. They appeared to be a very effective corps.

A desire by the government to create a more disciplined and controllable force caused Lord Castlereagh, the war minister, to propose an Act for the introduction of an obligation of universal military service in a Local Militia. This was apart from the general militia. Men were to be enrolled for four years, at the end of which they were free from the regular militia ballot for two years. This Act was responsible for the formation of three regiments of local militia in Northumberland. There was the Northern Regiment of Local Militia, commanded by Lieutenant Colonel Horace St Paul, formerly of the Royal Cheviot Legion, which would seem to indicate that the Cheviot had transferred to the local militia. Its headquarters was in Alnwick, and it consisted of ten companies with 761 privates, according to a return dated 21 February 1814. Second was the Western Regiment, with its headquarters at Hexham, under Lieutenant Colonel Commandant Thomas Wentworth Beaumont, with Lieutenant Colonel William Carr, formerly commanding the Hexham Volunteer Infantry. This was clearly another case of volunteers electing for the militia. A return dated 21 January 1814 shows ten companies of 788 private soldiers. The third was the Southern Regiment. Its return of 1 February 1814 shows that it consisted of ten companies of 765 soldiers, commanded by Colonel Commandant Charles William Bigge, with headquarters at Morpeth. It is of interest to note that the remains of the colours of the Southern Regiment of Northumberland Local Militia, which were laid up in St Michael's church, Alnwick, in 1818, are still hanging there today, though rather tattered.

Not all of the volunteers had opted to serve with the local militia. An abstract of muster rolls of corps and companies of yeomanry and volunteers within the counties of Northumberland, Newcastle-upon-Tyne, and the town of Berwick-upon-Tweed, dated 22 April 1812 (NRO), shows that the following volunteer units were still in existence:

Colours of the Southern Regiment of local militia. Laid up in St Michael's church, Alnwick, in 1818. (J. Winter)

Percy Tenantry Volunteer Cavalry	287
Horse Artillery attached to Cavalry	26
Percy Tenantry Volunteer Riflemen	1,195
Newcastle Loyal Associated Volunteer Infantry	756
Newcastle Volunteer Infantry	233
North Shields and Tynemouth Volunteer Infantry	262
Wallsend Volunteer Rifles	147
Bywell Volunteer Yeomanry Cavalry	76
Glendale Volunteer Infantry	69
Coquetdale Ranger Volunteer Cavalry	51
Berwick Artillery	64

The Bywell Cavalry had been raised in 1803 under Captain Commandant William Hodgson. In 1812 the commanding officer was Captain George Silvertop, with seventy-five troopers. This unit was still serving in 1819, under Captain John Cresswell Jobbing, with 139 serving members. There had also been the Slaley and Bywell-St Andrew's Volunteer Infantry formed in 1803 under Captain William Bainbridge with 139 serving members. As these would be rural agricultural areas, these numbers give some indication of the labour-intensive farming methods of farming during that period. Once again there is reason to suggest that with the conditions of employment – yearly contracts with tied housing – there may have been a sense of obligation to their employers, and a desire to escape service in the general militia, that lay apart from any feeling of patriotism that caused them to enrol in these small rural corps of volunteers.

Yet, according to Linda Colley in *Britons* (London, 1992), there were 15,222 men between the ages of seventeen and fifty-five in Northumberland in May 1804, of whom 6.96 per cent were volunteers, with 4,649 already in uniform in May 1804. This was 76 per cent of the total available, but she stresses that the figures may not be quite accurate. This percentage is only beaten by the county of Argyll, in Scotland, which shows 91 per cent. So there may have been a strong element of patriotism and loyalty in Northumberland and Newcastle, plus an element of independence passed down through the centuries from the Border Reivers and as a result of the constant strife with Scotland. Following the Treaty of Paris on 30 May 1814, broken for a short while by Napoleon's escape from Elba, an Order in Council was made on 6 July for a general disbandment of the volunteers. The local militias were not disbanded until 1818, after an Act 56. George III c.3. cancelled the militia ballot. As will be seen later, one of these volunteer corps remained together, and was to resurface again during the great patriotic upsurge of 1859-1860, when Great Britain was once again thought to be under threat of invasion by France.

THREE

THE NORTHUMBERLAND HUSSAR YEOMANRY: 'THE NOODLES'

At the auld Ridin Skyul he larned 'Reet Aboot',
But his knees they stuck in, and his toes they stuck oot,
His heart it was form, and as teuf as his belt,
So, defyin a' danger, to the Moor he did pelt.

Edward Corven, 1862.

In the summer of 1815, over twenty years of near-continuous war with France came to an end. Napoleon's defeat at Waterloo was a cause for celebration, but peace did not bring tranquillity at home. For many of the working people in Northumberland and Newcastle in the aftermath of the war, there was little to celebrate as life became harder. The economy had been geared for war for so long that the reduction in demand for arms, coupled with the demobilisation of men from the Army and Navy, caused a severe slump in trading conditions, manufacture and agriculture, leading to unemployment and a steep fall in wages which lasted into the early 1820s. This led to industrial unrest and agitation among the people for radical reform, especially among the pitmen and keelmen of Tyneside. The coal owners, industrialists, and those in commerce in Newcastle, together with the aristocratic and landowning gentry of rural Northumberland, were forced to take a long hard look at the situation.

The dramatic consequences of the French Revolution for the aristocrats and gentry of France led those of similar status in Great Britain to fear that the same fate might befall them, and they began to look for a means of ensuring the safety of their person and property. A revolutionary spirit was prevalent, particularly in the north, which had little regard for either public or private property, and protesters vented their anger and frustration in riots and a rapid increase in crime. Another cause for alarm was the Peterloo incident at Manchester, on 16 August 1819, which was perhaps a catalyst in the formation of a regiment of yeomanry from among the tenants and estate workers of the landowners, employees of the coal owners and small businessmen, who saw the social and political unrest as a threat to the stability of the area and to the safety of their interests. As Lord Lieutenant, the Duke of Northumberland saw fit to call a meeting of the magistrates of the county on 29 October 1819, to consider the best means of 'rendering effectual aid to the civil power in case of disturbance.'

Accordingly, in December 1819, the Northumberland and Newcastle Volunteer Corps of Cavalry, which included 'gentlemen of great respectability, such as merchants, brokers and tradesmen, together with officials of the collieries, and tenantry and retainers of the landed proprietors', was raised in Newcastle. It was under the command of Charles John Brandling of Gosforth House, formerly a Member of Parliament for Newcastle (1797–1812). Apart from his estates and coal interests in the North East, he owned collieries in Yorkshire. He was also involved with George Stephenson in the development of the railways. Six troops were formed: The Newcastle Troop; First Gosforth Troop; Second Gosforth Troop; Woolsington Troop; Backworth Troop; Willington Troop and a Troop of Dismounted Yeomanry.

A return dated 1 April 1823 (NRO) shows the Northumberland and Newcastle Yeomanry as being 254 strong. It is evident that local industry was strongly supportive of the unit as horses had been supplied by the following collieries: Willington; Felling; Gosforth; Kenton & Coxlodge; Hartley and Collingwood. The Tyne and Seaton Sluice Breweries had also provided horses. The five trumpeters' horses had come from: Dixon Brown (William Thompson); Gosforth Colliery (Joseph Boggen); John Smith's (his own); Wallsend Colliery (Thomas Roseby); Willington (Christopher Clarke). Of the twenty-two officers, only one had his horse supplied. He was Cornet George Johnson, whose horse came from Wallsend Colliery. It can be seen, therefore, that there were vested interests strongly involved, and it is reasonable to look upon the yeomanry at that time as tools of the employers.

From time to time the regiment was called out to assist in the maintenance of public order. In 1822, after its annual training, it remained on duty in aid of the civil powers for another twenty-three days, owing to strike riots among the keelmen on the river Tyne. On 24 October, seamen joined with keelmen who went upstream from Shields in boats, taking hostages from the crews loading coal on the river. The mayor, aided by special constables, took thirty prisoners from among the strikers. They were taken to the Castle of Newcastle, where a crowd of rioters called for their release. The approaches to the castle were guarded by the Yeomanry, and when the crowd became violent, the Riot Act was read. The strike ended at the beginning of December. A letter was received by the Duke of Northumberland from Robert Peel, the Home Secretary (1822–27), commending the regiment.

IT being thought expedient, at this Period, by many of the Inhabitants of this Town, to form an ARMED ASSOCIATION, for the Protection of Property, in Aid of the Civil Power; such Persons as wish to enrol themselves, for that Purpose, are informed, that they may enter their Names and Places of Residence in a Book, which will lie at the Exchange, Sandhill, until the 28th Instant in the Evening, when the List will be closed.

Newcastle, 25th October, 1819.

Recruiting poster for Northumberland and Newcastle Volunteer Cavalry.

> Dec. 12, 1822 – I have the honour to lay before the King your grace's letter, and I have received His Majesty's command to request that you will signify to Lieut.Colonel Brandling the great satisfaction which His Majesty derived from the zeal and discretion displayed by himself, the officers, non-commissioned officers, and privates of the Northumberland and Newcastle Yeomanry in aiding the civil power in their emergency.

An erroneous impression may be gained from the above as to the conduct of the members of the Yeomanry during the civil unrest, for there was another letter, revealed by Peter Cadogan in his *Early Radical Newcastle* (Consett, 1975). This was from John Buddle, agent to Lord Londonderry, a Durham coal owner:

> I have frequently seen the military called out in our pitmen and keelmen strikes both yeomanry and regular cavalry. The former were generally a laughing stock to the mob, while the latter were feared and respected. A painted staff [truncheon] with G.R. upon it is more awful in the hands of a special constable, than a sabre in the hands of the same individual, as a yeomanry man.

While there are grounds for crediting them with a sense of patriotism and good citizenship, it is worth considering that many of them may have been employed by their officers in a civilian capacity, therefore they may had some sense of obligation, even compulsion. It is also possible that some of them were sympathetic to the aspirations of the strikers. Called out again during the pitmens strike of 1831, the regiment was on permanent duty for thirty-three days. They were not involved during the political protest rallies of the radical Chartist movement, which lasted from 1838 until 1849, although armed regular troops of the Newcastle Garrison, from Newcastle Barracks, were actively involved.

These disturbances gradually abated, and the purely military function of the regiment for home defence and aid to the civil power took precedence, and with the setting up of a formed and disciplined police force in Newcastle, the civil power aspect became less important. Around this time, the annual training of eight days, held on the Town Moor, became one of the most important events in the social calendar of the upper-classes in the North East. As such, from the mid-nineteenth century, ceremonial and social roles accounted for the majority of the regiment's responsibilities. An instance of this involvement in the social life of Newcastle can be found in the pages of the local newspapers of the day. One newspaper, *The Morning Journal*, 9 October, reported that,

> The regiment was reviewed on the Town Moor by the Duke of Northumberland, who wore the full uniform of a Lord Lieutenant, complete with the insignia of the Order of the Garter. The weather being favourable there was a numerous assemblage of the

beau-monde on the ground to witness the spectacle; among others was Her Grace the Duchess of Northumberland, in a splendid equipage drawn by six beautiful blood horses.

The final social event of the annual training for that year was a grand ball in the Assembly Rooms, attended by, 'in all, 343 ladies and gentlemen, who included nearly the whole of the gentry of the neighbourhood'. The only breaks with this tradition between 1828 and the beginning of the Boer War, were in 1853, due to cholera, and 1877, owing to administrative problems. In 1847 John Dobson, the Newcastle architect, was commissioned to design a headquarters, riding school, armoury and stores, to be sited in Bath Street (now Northumberland Road). This building was completed in 1849, and was the headquarters of the regiment until 1954. It is now used by Northumbria University as an Information Technology Centre known as the Drill Hall.

Construction of the riding school facilitated mounted drill and riding instruction outside the annual eight days' training. The Yeomanry gradually spread its tentacles among the 'squirearchy' of the landowning, farming, hunting and shooting fraternity, and their retainers and tenants. This resulted in only one of the four squadrons being based in Newcastle. The other three were spread over an area stretching from Berwick in the north, to Darlington and Stockton in the south, and from Sunderland and Tynemouth in the east to Haltwhistle in the west.

The formation of the Rifle Volunteers in 1859–1860 caused some friction between the two corps. The yeomen were paid while the riflemen were not. A dialect song, 'The Noodle an' Rifleman's Dispute', written at the time by Joe Wilson, a well-known Newcastle entertainer, tells of the pay problem between them:

> The riflemen are volunteers withoot the daily pay,
> Thor services nivor bowt,
> Like the heroes of pipe clay!
> Amid the hoorays an' the deefnin cheers,
> This brave sowljer took his seat,
> Applauded biv a' Mackey's props,
> Expectin' he'd stand treat.

> The Noodles thor a' gentlemen,
> Rispected ti be sure,
> They nivor like the rifle curs,
> Fired ramrods on the Moor; The riflemen black-legged us a',
> undermin'd wor daily pay,
> But smash, aw'll fight him for a quart
> Then for waar, lads, clear the way.

This social comment indicates the tension that existed between those who regarded themselves as patriotic volunteers prepared to finance themselves as self-sufficient bodies of riflemen, and those who, perhaps, regarded those men of the Yeomanry as mercenaries. There was certainly a general contempt for the Yeomanry among the working people in the area in the first half of the nineteenth century, due to their involvement in quelling political and industrial dissent, hence the derogatory epithet of 'The Noodles':

> *Blue bummed bumblers,*
> *Cock-tail tumblers,*
> *Fireside sowjers,*
> *Dor'nt gan te waar.*

Some decidedly unlikely recruits joined the regiment as a result of this expansion. Troop-sized detachments were established in small rural and urban areas such as Ashington, which at that time was a rapidly expanding mining village in south-east Northumberland, eventually establishing a claim to be the largest mining village in the world. The troop was composed mainly of coal miners. It subsequently became one of best-recruited troops in the regiment. Such was the appeal of working with horses, and perhaps, the affiliation with some the most noted families in the North East. No doubt the lure of an extremely smart uniform would also have been an attraction for many young men. The financial aspect, and the kudos of belonging to an elite regiment, would have been added inducements to enlist. But patriotism and elitism aside, the annual training with pay, away from the dirty, dark and dangerous environment in which they worked, would have been a major attraction in the days before paid annual holidays became the norm.

It was the Boer War (1899–1900) which was to have a profound effect upon the Northumberland Yeomanry. Following the early reverses inflicted upon the British Army, it was realised that this was not going to be just another Imperial campaign and that many more mounted troops would be required. Mr Henry Scott, later knighted, of Hipsburn, near Alnwick, wrote to the local press on 18 December 1899, proposing that a mounted force of 100 volunteers should be raised in the county. He offered to contribute £1,000 to a fund to recruit and equip such a number. This was taken up by Earl Grey, then Lord Lieutenant of Northumberland. He contacted Lord Lansdowne, Secretary of State for War 1895–1900, supporting the proposal and also giving £1,000 to the fund. A group of some of the wealthiest and most influential men in Northumberland and Newcastle, in keeping with the Victorian ethos of philanthopy and civic pride – and perhaps a modicum of self interest – donated the same amounts; the officers of the Yeomanry donated £2,000. Other contributions brought the fund to the total of £33,658. In County Durham, the Earl of Durham took up the appeal and the total sum raised in Durham was £16,527, making a grand total of £50,185. A committee was formed to administer the fund. It was used to make grants to the wages fund to subsidise the volunteers. Equipment was purchased for the Elswick Battery, and life insurance purchased for the men of the three companies in 1900, and the men of the Elswick Battery – married men for £250, and single men for £100. The Volunteer Service Companies of the infantry battalions were also insured for the same sums. Disablement allowances were paid to wounded and sick Yeomanry and needy dependants were assisted.

The recruiting of Yeomanry volunteers started immediately. There was a rapid response from the young men of the North East. Volunteers applied at the Riding School where they had to undergo rigorous medical and practical tests in riding and shooting. Those men who brought their own horses were given £40 to compensate them. This would seem to indicate that some of them would have come from the upper and middle classes with a good proportion of them from the rural districts. Instead of the original number of 100, 355 mounted men were eventually enlisted; they formed the 14th, 15th, and 55th Squadrons of the Imperial Yeomanry.

Farriers at work at Rothbury annual camp. (T. Hewitson)

The experience gained during the war in South Africa influenced annual training, which was extended from eight to sixteen days. The Yeomanry, who had always done their annual training on Newcastle Town Moor, sought fresh fields where there was greater space for manoeuvre, and exchanged billets for tented encampments, which they found at Rothbury, where the camps were held from 1900 to 1904. No doubt Major, the Lord Armstrong, of the second succession, of Cragside near Rothbury, a serving officer of the regiment, had a hand in this. From 1905 to 1907 the camps were held at Walwick Grange at Fourstones, near Hexham in the Tyne Valley. It was in this decade that the regiment provided mounted escorts for King Edward VII and the Shah of Persia on their visits to Northumberland.

As with the militia, the Haldane Reforms of 1908 affected the 'Noodles', but in a decidedly different manner. The old distinctions between the Rifle Volunteers and the Yeomanry were now abolished. The Northumberland Hussar Yeomanry were given a new role. The strength of the unit on 31 October 1907 was 476. Under new legislation of 1907 (7 Edward VII C9):

> The Territorial and Reserve Forces Act to provide for the reorganisation of H. M. Forces and for that purpose to authorise the establishment of County Associations for raising and maintaining a Territorial Force; for amending the Acts relating to the Reserve Forces.

There were some teething problems with the new organisation, one of the foremost being that of pay. The Yeomanry were paid 7s (35p) per day in training, but the new rates, when harmonised with the volunteers, would effectively halve their pay. Significant opposition came from the county hierarchy who had officered and commanded the Yeomanry from its first formation, as it had with the militia. The commanding officers were concerned that they would lose their autonomy and become more accountable to the War Office. Eventually the differences were resolved and a more co-ordinated system of training and administration was developed.

The Territorials of Northumberland, Durham and North Yorks were to be part of the newly formed Northumbrian Division commanded by Lieutenant General R.S.S. Baden-Powell, the founder of the Boy Scout movement. This was to be one of the fourteen Cavalry Brigades, and fourteen Infantry Divisions, each with its own artillery and supporting units. These divisions were for home defence, yet many individuals chose to volunteer for Imperial Service. The cadet units, which had been raised in universities and grammar schools, became part of a new Officers Training Corps (OTC). Otley, in Yorkshire, was the site of the Yeomanry annual camp in 1914, just prior to the war.

Escort to the Shah of Persia at Cragside, Rothbury, home of Lord Armstrong. (T. Hewitson)

Escort to King Edward VII. (T. Hewitson)

Trooper P.C. Kane, Walwick Grange annual camp, 1912. (T. Hewitson)

It is not the intention of this account of the 'Weekend Warriors' to tell of their activities in that war. These have been adequately recorded in their regimental histories. But it seems apposite to tell of the weeks immediately after mobilisation. On 6 August 1914 the regiment was under the command of Lord Ridley of Blagdon Hall; 'A' Squadron was billeted in the Grand Stand on Gosforth Racecourse, 'B' Squadron at Castle Eden in Durham, with 'C' Squadron at Bedlington. 'B' and 'C' Squadrons soon joined the rest at Gosforth. On 11 September, the regiment was ordered to Lyndhurst, Hampshire. Major Cookson of Meldon Hall was now the commanding officer. The Northumberland Hussars sailed for Belgium as Divisional Cavalry to the 7th Division. Among them was Sergeant Johnstone Abercrombie, from Ashington, who was to become a legend among the troopers of 'C' Squadron. The author of this account can recall as a young boy in the 1930s, seeing him as Squadron Sergeant Major of 'C' Squadron, riding up Station Road to the Drill Hall in Council Road, with its full-size wooden horses used for mounted drill. 'Jonty', as everyone knew him, had first joined the Percy Artillery Volunteer Company in Ashington. When it was disbanded in 1903, he transferred to the Hussars, in which he served for over thirty years, being awarded the MBE and MM. Second and third line units were raised for the regiment, with the second line going to France in 1917; the third remained in England.

With the end of the war came the necessary reduction of the war-raised units. The Territorial Force was also disbanded. In February 1920 the reconstruction of the territorial regiments began. In a speech in December 1920, Winston Churchill stated: '… the Northumberland Hussars were the only unit in the Territorial Army to be complete and organised up to establishment.' This had been done in six months. The War Office decided to disband some mounted units of the British Army in 1921. Only the ten senior yeomanry regiments were to be retained, but the 'Noodles' were 14th in order of precedence. Friends in high places, and the reputation of the regiment, helped in gaining permission, on 17 May 1921, to recruit as one of the ten selected cavalry regiments of the 5th (Yorks & Notts) Cavalry Brigade. At this time there was a great deal of industrial and social unrest, and a national coal miners' strike started on 9 April 1921. Due to the international tension that had followed the Bolshevik Revolution in Russia, the government of the day was fearful of revolution in this country. Certainly, there was agitation by communists and other radical groups in Newcastle and the surrounding district. On the night of 8 April haystack fires occurred at the Colliery Farm, Bedlington Station, Kitty Brewster, near Blyth, North Seaton Colliery and Bebside Colliery Farm. A hangar on the disused RAF Aerodrome on Newcastle Town Moor was also destroyed by fire. These must have been organised and concerted attacks. As a result of this unrest and disruption, reservists were called up, and 250 Royal Navy officers and ratings were stationed in Fenham Barracks, Newcastle, ready to help maintain essential services.

Ashington Troop, c.1911. (T. Hewitson)

The government decided to form a Volunteer Defence Force recruited from civilians and members of the Territorial Army to defend key points, and deny dissidents arms and ammunition. Territorials who volunteered for the force were discharged, and then enlisted in the new Defence Force. In this way the government circumnavigated laws relating to the use of territorials in industrial disputes. For the Hussars in Newcastle, headquarters were established in the Riding School on 9 June, and the building was strengthened as well, seeing barbed-wire defences erected. Accommodation for two squadrons was set up in 7 Saville Place, and one in the Riding School. Horses were borrowed from the Royal Artillery in Fenham Barracks, which allowed mounted training to take place. From 7 June two twenty-four-hour guards were mounted on the Tyne, Swing, and the Redheugh Bridges. The *Illustrated Chronicle*, 13 July 1921, reported that, in answer to a question by Mr Gratten Doyle, Conservative Unionist MP for Newcastle North, Sir L. Worthington replied: 'The total number of officers and men stationed in the coalfields during the recent dispute was approximately 12,000. The fact that these troops had been called upon to assist the civil powers had the effect of maintaining order.' The Defence Force was disbanded after a short period.

Hussars who had volunteered for Imperial service, pre-1914. Fifteen of them are wearing the silver Imperial Service Badge above the right pocket of tunic. (T. Hewitson)

Just before the First World War. (T. Hewitson)

Annual camp for 1922 was set up on the Pastures, opposite Alnwick Castle, on 17 June. A notable event for twenty Hussars of 'C' Squadron, who formed a Guard of Honour, commanded by Captain Eustace Smith MC, which took place on 10 August when Field Marshal Earl Haig visited Ashington in support of the British Legion. He had a full day of engagements in the mining village. His first was a speech to ex-servicemen in the now-vanished Miners Theatre, and he then inspected ex-servicemen in Portland Park football ground. In the evening he opened a ball in the Princess Ballroom, also vanished, which was followed by a dinner in the Portland Hotel. He ended his day by visiting the Comrades Social Club. The visit was reported in the *Newcastle Daily Journal*, 11 August 1922.

The annual cycle of training began again, culminating with the annual camp. Camp was by no means an easy period for the Yeomanry soldiers. As well as looking after their personal needs and equipment, they also had the responsibility of looking after a horse, which had to be fed, watered two or three times a day, groomed, and have all its saddlery maintained. Troop horses were provided by contractors, the officers usually bringing their own mounts with them. Many of the troopers had no experience of working with horses, although many of those who worked in the coal mines had worked underground with pit ponies. The annual camps of the inter-war period were held in the northern counties of Northumberland, Durham and Yorkshire, apart from 1926 because of the General Strike, and 1932 due to a national financial crisis, when no territorial camps were held. Obviously, the very nature of a mounted cavalry unit meant that these camps were not held with a view to off-duty time among the bright lights of a vibrant town. The locations of the camps precluded any such distractions. One of the most interesting and spectacular camps must have been the Cavalry Brigade camp held at Haltwhistle in 1936. The Northumberland Hussars, Yorkshire Hussars, Yorkshire Dragoons, Sherwood Rangers and 26 Armoured Car Company (East Riding Yeomanry), would have presented a splendid sight when they all paraded together. Social life between the various units would have also been quite lively. In the spring of 1939 the Northumberland Hussars were allowed to recruit up to war strength and went into annual camp at Welbeck Abbey with the Sherwood Rangers, making two fully recruited war strength regiments.

On 1 September 1939 the 'Noodles' received orders to mobilise. Once again the rendezvous for the regiment was Gosforth Park Racecourse, where the troopers arrived armed with a rifle and a sword. The Grandstand was used as accommodation for the bulk of the troopers, and the officers' mess was in a hut that had been the police dining room. The Orderly Room was in the weighing-in room and the canteen had been the Champagne Bar. As in the early stages of the 1914 mobilisation, Tilley's of Newcastle were involved in the catering arrangements. After three weeks at Gosforth Park, the regiment moved to Yorkshire. Headquarters were in Thorton-le-Dale, 'A' Squadron at Pickering, 'B' at Wydale, and 'C' at Dalby. It was here that horses were issued. In the last two months of 1939 the regiment moved by squadrons to Louth in Lincolnshire. Extensive reorganisations of the cavalry occurred in this period. Brigaded cavalry regiments were to go to Palestine, and non-brigaded cavalry regiments were to turn their horse over to these units. Thus it was that the Northumberland Hussars lost their horses. All the paraphernalia, including spurs, bandolier, sword and saddlery were dispensed with.

Out of fifteen mounted yeomanry regiments, seven remained in England. Six of them became either Medium or Field Artillery. The Northumberlands converted to an anti-tank regiment. The official date of the change of designation was 15 February 1940, and their new title was 102nd (Northumberland) Light Anti-Aircraft and Anti-Tank Regiment, Royal Artillery. The regiment was allowed to retain its old cap badge. Moving to Northampton in June, the regiment became part of the 2nd Armoured Division. In mid-November

Right: *Trooper Bill Parry of Ashington 'C' Squadron, 1939. (T. Hewitson)*

Below: *A troop HQ of 'C' Squadron, Ashington. The officer on the left is Hugh Percy, later 10th Duke of Northumberland. The trooper on the right is Bill Parry of Ashington, c.1939. (T. Hewitson)*

1940, the regiment sailed from Liverpool for the Middle East and war. In 1941 the regiment was reduced from four to three batteries, losing its anti-aircraft role to 15th Light Anti-Aircraft Regiment, Royal Artillery. This battery was re-designated as 247th (Northumberland Hussars) Light Anti-Aircraft Battery, Royal Artillery.

With the end of the war in 1945, the Territorial Army was disbanded along with the temporary war-raised units, and some regular units were placed in suspended animation. In the autumn of 1946 it was announced that the Territorial Army was to be reconstituted, and the Northumberland Hussars were to be reformed as 50th (Northumbrian) Divisional Reconnaissance Regiment (TA). On 11 January 1947, the regiment was affiliated to the 15th/19th King's Royal Hussars. Lieutenant Colonel Eustace Smith was appointed as commanding officer, and an adjutant and quartermaster were seconded from the 15th/19th. It was not until May 1948 that serious recruiting was undertaken. In Hyde Park, on Sunday 31 October 1948, King George VI reviewed 8,000 members from every unit of the Territorial Army, including eighty women from the Auxiliary Territorial Service (ATS) and fifty-two aircraft of the Royal Auxiliary Air Force (RAAF). The Royal Naval Volunteer Reserve (RNVR) took part in the flypast. The hussar squadrons were relocated in their old recruiting areas. Regimental Headquarters, 'A' Squadron and Headquarter Squadron re-occupied the Riding School in Northumberland Road, Newcastle. 'B' Squadron were located in the Drill Hall in Collingwood Street, South Shields. 'C' Squadron, with a troop based in the Duke's School, Alnwick, were located in the Drill Hall on Council Road, Ashington, along with 'B' and 'S' Companies of the 7th/Royal Northumberland Fusiliers (TA). As with most units of the TA at this time, recruits were slow to come forward. Many young men were awaiting release from the services, and due to National Service (conscription) the traditional recruits were not available. As a consequence, many coal miners, still officially in a reserved occupation, were enrolled.

One of those who enlisted was Tom Bacon, a blacksmith at Ashington Colliery. He wrote in the *Creeful of Coals* (Newbiggin, April 2001):

I was approached by Jimmy Richardson the manager of the Machine Shop. He had been Squadron Sergeant Major of 'C' Squadron, and a Prisoner of War (PoW) in Germany. Jimmy spoke with a voice that sounded as if he had swallowed a mouthful of gravel. He said: 'Young Bacon – ye hev ti report for a medical at sivin o'clock at thi Drill Haall on Cooncil Road, on Friday neet. Yaar in thi hussars.' 'O aye', aa says, 'and waat if aa divven't want ti join yaa hussars?' He replied, 'Yaa faather was a hussar – yor ganna be one n'aal'. Jimmy ticked my name off his list and went to order some more to join, nine in all.

Other blacksmiths who were inveigled into joining by Jimmy Richardson, were Geordie Shearer, Tom Mears, Dennis Crate, Hedley Parsons, Stevie Richardson, Tommy Lockyer, Tommy Johnson, Jimmy Chapman and Jack Abercrombie, nephew of 'Jonty' Abercrombie, the pre-war SSM. Among others who enlisted were former wartime members of the regiment. It was the return of National Servicemen who were committed to four year's part-time service after completing their full-time service, which eventually made a difference to the strength of the regiment, as it did to all TA units.

The regiment, in the role of Divisional Reconnaissance, was issued with Cromwell tanks from 1946 to 1949. In the initial stages, 'C' Squadron had difficulties housing their two tanks. One was kept in a hut on the golf course at Newbiggin, while the other was kept at the home of Lord Richard Percy at Lesbury, near Alnwick. All the squadrons seemed to have trouble finding adequate garaging for their tanks. The first post-war annual camp was held in 1948 at Streatlam Camp, at Barnard Castle, County Durham with the 7th Hussars, and again in 1949. The diversity of camp locations after the war meant that the opportunity for travel away from the North East was enhanced. In 1950 the regiment was given a new role, that of an anti-tank unit, exactly the role they had been engaged in during the latter stages of the war. They were issued with self-propelled, 17-pounder anti-tank guns mounted on a Valentine tank chassis, and their annual camp in this role was held at Windmill Hill, Tidworth.

Due to the deteriorating international situation, exacerbated by the war in Korea, which lasted from 1950 to 1953, the government of 1951 decided to call up Class 'Z' army reservists for two weeks' training with Territorial Army units. Each unit would be brought up to full wartime establishment and 1st Line Reserves. Over 500 reservists joined the hussars at Kircudbright, Scotland, for their attachment. That year also saw a number of changes to the home locations of the squadrons of the regiment. 'C' Squadron moved into a brand new Drill Hall in Lintonville Terrace, which is now a carpet showroom. The old Riding School in Newcastle and the Drill Hall in South Shields were both renovated and extended. Many of the old regimental traditions were resumed and the extremely active social life, for which the regiment was famous, became once more a focal point for a lot of the county and city society. The Coronation of Queen Elizabeth II in June 1953 was a great ceremonial occasion in which the regiment played their part. Two detachments were sent to London, one for the procession party and one for route-lining. In the Newcastle celebration parade on 6 June, the regiment provided four detachments, one of four mounted officers in full dress, a marching detachment of sixty-eight of all ranks, and in the rear, a Cromwell tank and two Valentine tanks. The regimental band, under Bandmaster Sugget, played at the saluting base at Barrass Bridge.

It was in 1953 that the first full-scale divisional exercise since the end of the war, took place on Salisbury Plain. All the units of 50 (Northumbrian) Division were scattered in various locations, the Hussars with 150 Brigade at Tilshead. I, then a twenty-one year old territorial fusilier, with 'B' Company, 7/RNF, had spent a couple of days sitting in a shell hole on Imber Artillery Range with nothing to eat during the exercise, as our Colour Sergeant, and our rations, had been captured by the opposing forces. Then with a roaring engine and the clanking of tracks, a Valentine self-propelled 17-pounder anti-tank gun carrier, drove up and parked close to my particular shell hole. I said 'bugger the war', or words to that effect, jumped out of my shell hole and asked the crew of 'Noodles' if they had anything to eat. They kindly gave me a vast amount of composite ration hard-tack biscuits, which really were hard and had the consistency of rolled steel plate, which they didn't want anyway, as well as some tins of compo cheese. Lastly, and most importantly, they offered a tin-opener. These I gratefully accepted and went back to the shell hole to share my booty with the rest of my section. They demanded to know why I had not managed to get some tins of stewed steak.

A year later there was a wholesale change in the location of the squadrons. Regimental Headquarters and 'A' Squadron moved out of the Riding School into new quarters at Debden Gardens in Heaton, Newcastle, and, in November, 'B' Squadron into Frenchman's Fort. In 1955 the regiment was once again given a new armoured role and equipped with Comet tanks, which started to arrive in February. In May there was a re-think, and the tank role was forgotten. They were to be issued with armoured and scout cars. This decade was one of constant change and economic cutbacks which affected not only the 'Noodles', but all the other TA units in the North East. Then yet another change, this time into a reconaissance role – each change making it less and less effective in a military role with more emphasis on aid to the civil power – with training at the Civil Defence Headquarters at Darras Hall, near Ponteland. The last compulsory annual training for National Servicemen was held in 1956 and, from that year onwards, the TA was composed completely of volunteers. Serious efforts had to be made to recruit volunteers to replace the NS men who did not wish to stay with the regiment. With this in mind, annual camp was held in Hexham, and concentrated publicity within the two counties of Northumberland and Durham. As a sign of the times, the first part of the Camp was devoted to civil defence training.

A significant event in the history of the Territorial Army took place in 1958. This was the Golden Jubilee of the Territorial Army. On Sunday 22 June, during a violent thunderstorm, a party of thirty of all ranks, under the command of Major the Honourable W.M. Ridley, took part in a parade in Hyde Park, London, where Her Majesty Queen Elizabeth II reviewed contingents from units in the Territorial Army. Newcastle and Northumberland Territorials held their own parade on Saturday 5 July, with all the TA units in the area represented. The parade formed up on the infantry square of Fenham Barracks and was inspected by the Duke of Northumberland, Lord Lieutenant of the county. They then marched through the city. Another memorable ceremony in the history of the regiment took place on the rain-sodden infantry square of Fenham Barracks on Saturday 30 September 1961. This was for the presentation of a new guidon to the regiment, under the command of Lieutenant Colonel Lord Richard Percy, by his brother the Duke of Northumberland, who had also been a serving officer in the regiment. The dark and sombre atmosphere was illuminated by the striking scarlet caps, yellow striped overalls and gleaming spurs of the bandsmen of the 15th/19th Hussars, and the elegant Cambridge blue banded caps and glittering chain-mail epaulettes of the No.1 dress blues worn by the two dismounted guards of Northumberland's. A vehicle squadron with the crews in khaki battledress was drawn up behind the two guards. Three officers, arrayed in the full dress uniforms of the Victorian period, riding beautifully groomed chargers adorned with leopard skin shabraques (saddle cloths), preceded the duke while he inspected the regiment. The guidon party consisted of three squadron sergeant majors, with SSM W.A. Willis of 'C' Squadron bearing the new guidon. From the barracks, the regiment, led by the band, marched down into the city, passing the saluting base at Eldon Square, where the duke took the salute. Shortly after this, Lord Percy relinquished command and Lieutenant Colonel the Honourable M.W. Ridley replaced him. He was the fourth member of his family to command the regiment.

In 1962, a year of financial stringency on the part of the government, there were further cuts in funding for the TA. One innovation was the establishment of the Territorial Army Emergency Reserve (TAER), or 'Ever Readies' as they were labelled. Those who volunteered were liable to be called out at any time, and anywhere, for six-month service. For this they received a taxable bounty of £150 per year, and £50 tax free for each call out. One sergeant and two corporals from the regiment went out to Aden for two weeks training with the 10th Hussars. Annual camp for 1962 was held in Scotland, and the annual tradition of an officers' box at the Newcastle Race Meeting was honoured by a visit from the Queen Mother on 30 June. Elements of the regiment took part in Exercise *Overlord II* which took place on Holy Island, off the coast of Northumberland, on 29–30 September. Units from the RNF, KOSB, RMVR, RNVR, RA, RE, RCT and RAF were also involved. Striking headlines

Northumberland Hussars Yeomanry

Headquarters:
NEWCASTLE-ON-TYNE.

The Regiment was raised in 1819 as the Northumberland and Newcastle Volunteer Cavalry, its first Commanding Officer being Colonel C. J. Brandling. When first formed, 20 men of each troop were armed with carbines and trained as light infantry, and this organisation continued until 1876, when the War Office decided that the functions of Yeomanry Regiments should be exclusively devoted to those of light cavalry.

At the same time the designation of the Regiment was changed to that of " The Northumberland (Hussars) Yeomanry Cavalry." During the South African war the gallant spirit of the men of both Tyneside and Wearside was shown by the large number of officers and men who volunteered for service with the various Imperial Yeomanry Contingents who proceeded to the front to fight the battles of their Country, many of whom distinguished themselves in several actions, notably those at Rooidam, Hartebeestfontein, Springkop, and Zeerust. The Regiment won fame in the present great war by the splendid courage and perseverance of all ranks who went to the front with the famous 7th Division, and helped to hold up the enemy in the most critical stage of the war. They were mentioned in dispatches for their f ne discipline and bearing, which were described as favourably comparing with the Regulars.

Published during the First World War.

in the *Newcastle Journal* stated, 'Terriers drink the Island dry'. This was no exaggeration. There were some pretty seedy-looking territorial soldiers on the Sunday morning. But the exercise commenced anyway, and the ensuing scene of soldiers charging about to a background of cracks, bangs and blank rifle-fire, with planes zooming overhead, provided an unusual diversion for the tourists on the island, the seat of Christianity in the British Isles, and home of the Lindisfarne Gospels.

Camp for 1963 was held in Sussex. In 1964, Camp was at Warcop, Westmoreland, and, in 1965, Norfolk. It was in December 1965 that a government white paper – 'Reorganisation of the Army Reserves' – was published, which was to have dramatic consequences for the Territorial Army. In essence, it was a complete reassessment of the organisation of the TA, which saw many regiments, such as the 'Noodles', with so many years service, reduced to a small cadre and, in some cases, disbanded. The Reserve Forces Act of 1966 followed the reorganisation of the TA in 1960, The Act of 1962, which introduced the 'Ever Readies', and the Act of 1964 which created a long-term reserve for ex-regulars. As it stated in Clause 3 of The White Paper:

It is no longer realistic to maintain ground forces designed to fight another major conventional war of large armies in Europe. The risk of major war in Europe is now small but if it did come it would involve the use of nuclear weapons. This is the basis of the Western Alliance strategy. Clause 5 maintained: Over recent years there has been built up a volunteer Regular Army which contains a high proportion of fighting units with insufficient logistic units to meet the requirements of major military operations overseas.

After all the upheaval and decimation of both the TA and the Regular Army, carried out by governments led by both political parties, the situation today, as far as the defence of the British Isles is concerned, is worse than ever. In January 1968 it was the government's decision to disband Civil Defence, Auxiliary Fire Service and all T & AVR III Units. The regiment, or what was left of it, went into a week's camp at Tidworth, which was unpaid. There had been discussions with a view to amalgamating with 101 Medium Regiment RA (V), which had been retained in a T & AVR II role, but this did not transpire. The 'Noodles' elected to disband. The City of Newcastle conferred the Freedom of the City upon the regiment to mark the 150th anniversary of its formation in 1819. The presentation was held in the Civic Centre on 15 March 1969, with all the ceremonial and dignity befitting such an auspicious occasion, enhanced by the presence of the Regimental Band of the 15th/19th Hussars, when the Lord mayor presented the Freedom Scroll to the Honorary Colonel, and Viscount Ridley, Chairman of Northumberland County Council, presented a Resolution from the County Council, recognising the part played by the regiment over the last 150 years.

As from 1 April 1969, the Northumberland Hussars consisted of a cadre of three officers and five troopers. They were attached to 101 (N) Medium Regiment RA (TA) based in the Drill Hall on Barrack Road - now converted into apartments - for administrative purposes. This cadre lasted for two years. Following the election of a Conservative Government in 1970, pledges were made to increase the size of the T & AVR. It was announced that a new Armoured Car Regiment was to be formed, made up from the existing cadres of the various yeomanry regiments, and would consist of three sabre squadrons and one headquarters squadron. A Ministry of Defence Instruction, 'Expansion of the Territorial Army and Volunteer Reserve', dated 29 January 1971, was the catalyst for the creation of this new unit. On 1 March 1971, moves were made to create what was eventually to become The Queen's Own Yeomanry. The administrative centre of the new regiment, which was spread over a huge geographical area, was to be in Tynemouth, with Headquarters

Squadron being formed from the old Northumberland Hussars. So from this time on, the 'Noodles' were no longer to be a major regiment in the British Army Order of Battle. As far as the North East was concerned, it was now a sub-unit of an amalgamated yeomanry regiment. This regiment was to embrace the long history and traditions of four famous Territorial Cavalry Regiments: the Ayrshire, Cheshire, Northumberland, and Yorkshire Yeomanry. Now, headquarters are based in Fenham Barracks, Newcastle. In 1969 the 'Noodles' disappeared; whether their successors will still be there in 2009 is anyone's guess.

FOUR

The Rifle Volunteers

*We are the **2**nd Northumberland,*
Some thought we were the worst,
But after the inspection,
I think we should be first;
And if the Queen wants good men,
Her enemies to kill,
We are the lads at Hexham,
For we all know our drill.

Bugler Thomas Robson, Hexham.

Britain in the mid-nineteenth century was at the zenith of its imperial power. The Great Exhibition of 1851 had displayed to the rest of the world the wealth and power of the first great modern industrialised nation. Many people had prospered on the crest of this industrial upsurge, and a new middle class had been born. An example of this Victorian powerhouse was industrial Tyneside. A major exercise in civil engineering began with the formation of the Tyne Improvement Commission in 1850. This massive project involved the dredging of the river Tyne. Hitherto, the river had been barely navigable, and the coal was transported by shallow keelboats to the colliers waiting downstream in the river estuary.

The dredging of the upper reaches which commenced in 1861, and the erection of the Swing Bridge which opened to pedestrian and vehicular traffic in June 1876, enabled deep draught vessels to berth at Newcastle Quayside. A rapidly expanding railway system, first developed in the North East, was beginning to create a web of communications between previously isolated communities. All this development was to change the face of Tyneside and, as a consequence, bring enormous economic benefits to an oligarchy of the aristocracy, landowners, coal owners, industrialists and those in commerce in the area. Unfortunately, these enormous economic benefits did not always filter down to the poorer labouring class. On the other hand, a great deal of employment was created as the industry flourished along the riverside. Another factor was the influx of Scots and Irish into the North East, keen to take advantage of the new employment opportunities.

The idea of Britain as a mighty world power, as projected by the Great Exhibition, was flawed in terms of military potential. The main factor was that the Regular Army could only sustain its role in providing adequate forces to protect the Empire by depleting the home defences, precisely what is happening today in the twenty-first century. An added problem was the lack of recruits for the army. This had been exacerbated by the wholesale migration of Irish people to America, Canada and Australia, indeed anywhere where they could start a new life after the potato famines of the 1840s in Ireland.

Not even the militia revival in 1852 could calm the sense of unease felt by many of the military and political establishment. As early as 1848, the Duke of Wellington was voicing his doubts about the capacity of the home forces to repel an invader. In 1852 General Sir Charles Napier addressed a letter to the House of Commons, proposing a solution for the defence of Britain during the absence overseas of the Regular Army by the establishment of an armed force of volunteer corps and militia. Both approaches were ignored by the government. The exposure by William Russell, special correspondent for *The Times*, of the administrative inadequacies of the army during the Crimean War (1854–1856) and the Indian Mutiny (1857–1858), as well as the ineptitude of the army at home, brought about the realisation that Britain's land-based defences were totally inadequate.

A war launched against Austria by Louis Napoleon, Napoleon III, (1851–1873) in May 1859, caused the Prime Minister, Lord Palmerston, to mobilise the militia. Even though there was a sustained press campaign, led by *The Times*, which urged the government to adopt the idea of a Volunteer Force, the government and some military leaders still raised objections. The Duke of Cambridge wrote:

> I dismiss at once from my mind, all the ideas in public prints about the volunteer corps. If such a system were to be adopted the spirit of the Regular Army would be destroyed and jealousies would at once be engendered. Volunteers would do as much or as little as they liked, and in fact they would be an armed and very dangerous rabble.

Hugh Cunningham, in *The Volunteer Force* (London, 1975), suggested that there was no sign of any great public enthusiasm for the Force at this time. There seemed to be more of an emphasis on maintaining the Channel Fleet.

On Monday 9 May 1859, *The Times* published a patriotic poem, *Riflemen Form* by Lord Tennyson, the Poet Laureate. This was a seen as a patriotic rallying cry to the upper-and middle-class readership. One of the main reasons generally advanced to explain the response in 1859 to the call to join the Rifle Volunteers, was the incident concerning the assassination attempt upon the life of Louis Napoleon by Felice Orsini on 14 January 1858. The reaction of the French to the supposed British involvement created a sense of crisis and, on 12 May, a War Office circular was sent to the Lords Lieutenant of the counties, authorising the raising of a Volunteer Force. It was to be raised under the provisions of the 1804 Act, which had consolidated previous Acts relating to the volunteers of the Revolutionary and Napoleonic period (1793–1815). The War Office visualised an organisation along the lines of the Act, but there was one fundamental difference: members of any corps raised had to undertake to provide their own arms and equipment and bear all the expenses of themselves and their unit.

These clauses were quite clearly designed to restrict membership to those who could afford the outlay and who would not, under normal circumstances, consider service in the militia, yeomanry, or the Regular Army. Those who could not meet these requirements but wished to carry out some sort of military service would still be available as a recruiting source. In Northumberland and Newcastle, the reaction to the press campaign and patriotic rhetoric from influential members of the various communities led to a spate of General Meetings for those interested in the idea of volunteering. The financial restrictions meant that the labouring classes and poorer members of society who were unable to finance themselves were initially excluded from any such involvement.

Meetings were held in most towns and villages throughout the Tyne to Tweed area. The *Newcastle Journal*, 10 December 1859 reported that meetings had been held in Warkworth, Hexham, Berwick, and also that:

> The usual monthly meeting of the Newcastle Rifle Corps was held in the Riding School, on Wednesday evening last. Ninety-six new members, including the Highland sub-division, were elected. Sir John Fife, amid loud acclamation, was re-elected as senior officer. He stated that the corps now numbered seven companies and an eighth was in the course of formation. Three of these were original companies, two from the workmen and others from Messrs., Stephenson and Co., manufactury, and one from the works of Sir W.G. Armstrong and Co. Sir W.G. Armstrong has nominated as officers of his company Mr J.D. Scott as Lieutenant, and Mr C. Croudace as Ensign. The companies Sir John mentioned were the Temperance, Kilted, Quayside, Oddfellows, Guards, and a company drawn from the Hampton Factory, as well as those listed above.

In nearly every case, the meetings had been under the chairmanship of local dignitaries who would have had some influence in county affairs. The example of Sir W.G. Armstrong, founder of the Elswick works, shows the influence of patronage on the selection of officers. Another example was that of the Duke of Northumberland, who placed two cottages and Percy Square, in North Shields, at the disposal of the 1st Northumberland Volunteers (Tynemouth) for the purpose of drilling. The mention of the Highland sub-division is indicative of what was later to become a significant Scottish involvement in the auxiliary units of the North East. The Irish at this time do not seem to have become involved. There were legitimate reasons why they would resist such appeals. Sir Joseph Cowen, the radical MP, in a speech in Newcastle Town Hall on 3 January 1881, said:

> The Irishman's troubles are not listened to and his miseries have been mocked. The unsympathetic snarl with which the English press usually receives Irish proposals for a reform, tends to embitter the relations between the two peoples. Our illustrated papers seldom portray an Irish peasant in any other character except that of a scoundrel, a skulk, or a coward.

It is hardly surprising that with this type of discrimination the Irish community did not want to become involved. They would have also been discouraged by the financial implications.

On 17 December 1859 an advertisement appeared in the *Newcastle Journal* which gives us some idea of the social composition of the volunteer units, at least in Newcastle, during this initial period:

> In order to increase the strength and efficiency of this Corps, the Committee have determined upon the immediate formation of an additional company, to consist of Tradesmen, Clerks, and others, who shall provide their own Uniform and Accoutrements, and otherwise conform to the Rules and Regulations of the Corps, such Company to be provided with Government Rifles free of cost. Lists for the signature of those Parties wishing to join the above Company lie at the office of the Secretary, Barras Bridge, and at the Riding School, Northumberland Street. The Public are respectfully informed that, owing to the increased number of Gentlemen Drilling in the Riding School, Visitors will only be admitted when introduce by members.

Newcastle, although an urban area, was relatively slow to recruit in the initial stages, and embraced infantry, artillery and engineer units. This poor start may have had its roots in the opposition in some quarters to the volunteers in the North of England, and this is mentioned in the *Volunteer Service Gazette*, 28 January 1860. According to Revd Doctor J.G. Bruce, the local historian, the

ARMED ASSOCIATION.

At a General Meeting of the Special Constables of the Borough of Newcastle upon Tyne, held in the Lecture Room in Nelson Street, on Friday the 9th Day of August, 1839,

JOHN FIFE, Esquire, Mayor, in the Chair :

The following Resolutions

WERE UNANIMOUSLY ADOPTED:

1st. That, without reference to any political Object or Party, this Meeting form an **ARMED ASSOCIATION** for the Maintenance of the Authority of the Laws, and the Protection of Life and Property.

2nd. That those Gentlemen who cannot conveniently join the proposed Armed Association, be requested to continue their Services as **SPECIAL CONSTABLES.**

3rd. That both Bodies, the Military and Constabulary, do increase their Number; and that correct Lists of their respective Forces be forwarded to the Mayor, as early as possible.

4th. That a Committee be now appointed to carry out the Objects of the above Resolutions; and that such Committee consist of the following Gentlemen, viz.: The Mayor and Magistrates, Colonel CAMPBELL, the present Officers of the Constabulary Force, together with Doctors KNOTT and EMBLETON, and Mr R. M. GLOVER, with Power to add to their Number.

JOHN FIFE, Mayor, Chairman.

☞ A List is open at the POLICE STATION HOUSE, in the MANORS, for Gentlemen who wish to enrol themselves; where the Regulations may be seen.

Wm. Heaton, Printer, Newcastle.

'Fife's Poster'. (Courtesy of Newcastle Central Library)

first corps to be formed in Newcastle was the 1st Newcastle Rifle Volunteers, under the command of Lieutenant Colonel Sir John Fife, who had, for a long time, been an advocate of such a force. While he was mayor of the town in August 1839, during the period of Chartist agitation, he had proposed the formation of an Armed Association: 'For the Maintenance of the Authority of the Laws and the Protection of Life and Property'.

Sir John may seem a strange person to have advocated the formation of such a body of men, considering the fact that he was, for thirty years, a surgeon at Newcastle Infirmary, and that as an eye surgeon he had set up, together with a Mr T.M. Greenhow, a medical charity in Brunswick Place, known in later years as the Newcastle Eye Infirmary. However, in his civil life he was deeply involved in local politics and, as Sheriff of Newcastle, had been very robust in his dealings with social disorder in the town. A radical, he was one of the leading lights of the Northern Political Union, and an advocate of the Reform Bill. In 1838 he was elected mayor. But the Chartist agitation in the summer of 1839 forced him, as Chief Magistrate, to intervene in the disorders, ordering the armed troops from the local barracks to break up the demonstrations, which was done at the point of the bayonet. Twenty years later he had achieved his ambition and was commanding his own armed body.

One of the advantages of an urban unit was the social cohesion of the membership. These units would have been composed of like-minded individuals. But rather than patriotic sentiments, perhaps advancement in their working environment, social aspirations and peer pressure may have been more likely factors in their decision to enlist in a particular company. The first Annual General Meeting of the Newcastle Corps was held in the Riding School, Headquarters of the Northumberland Yeomanry, on Wednesday 9 May 1860. Lieutenant Thomas Grey, the paymaster to the Corps, stated that it had been founded:

> ... at a public meeting where forty-six gentlemen at once became members, and having obtained the requisite consent of the magistrates, commenced drilling under the instruction of Sergeant Smellie, in an enclosed piece of ground in Bath Lane, which, by an outlay of £13.00 they succeeded in making a very available drill ground. They continued there until the winter, when, by the kind consent of Captain Woods, they obtained use of the Riding School.

Due to increased interest in the Rifle Volunteers, and increasing numbers, the members set about acquiring uniforms and weapons. They adopted a steel-grey uniform with black braid, and received tenders for the supply of rifles from William Greener of Birmingham, formerly of Newcastle, at a cost of £4 10s (£4.50p).

In rural Northumberland, the market towns and outlying villages were the source of a number of Rifle Volunteer Corps. Meetings were held in December 1859 with the object of forming volunteer companies at Warkworth, Hexham, Morpeth and Berwick, where it was proposed to form a company to be called the Second Company of Northumberland Artillery and Rifle Volunteers; over 120 young men had already enrolled. These early companies were composed initially of the new middle class, such as the local doctor, schoolmaster, self-employed tradesmen, shopkeepers, and local businessmen. Local dignitaries would usually be elected by the members as officers of the corps, with the local vicar giving his full support. The wives and families of the members helped with frequent bazaars, fêtes, picnics, balls and other social and fundraising activities in support of their particular corps. Events such as these were beloved of the volunteers and their wives.

An account of a social occasion which appeared in the *Newcastle Courant*, 2 November 1860, gives us an indication of the changes and expansion Newcastle-upon-Tyne witnessed over 145 years:

WALKER:- The officers and volunteers of the Walker of the 1st Northumberland Rifles, held their first annual ball on Friday in the schoolrooms belonging to Messrs Losh, Wilson, and Bell, in that village, kindly lent for the occasion. They were established in the January of the present year. The officers are Captains Henry Bell of Whitley House, B.J. Thompson and William Swan; Lieutenants Swan, Latimer, and Lawton, Ensigns Crooke, Crawford and Jobling. They have been drilled by Sergeant Belcher, formerly of the Coldstream Guards. The arrangements for the ball had been made on a liberal and extensive scale; the ballroom ante-rooms, and refreshment rooms, being suitably and tastefully decorated. In the last named department tea and coffee, with accompaniments, were supplied by Mr Stirling, Westgate, Newcastle, while other refreshments were supplied Mr Tweddle of the *Ellison Arms,* St Anthony's. The company commenced to arrive at a few minutes before eight o'clock. A quadrille band conducted by Mr Clark, bandmaster of the corps, occupied a temporary orchestra (stage). Amongst those present were Captain H. Bell and Mrs Bell, Lieutenant J. Shield, Newcastle Company of the 1st Northumberland Volunteer Artillery, Captain Scott, Newcastle Rifles, and Mrs Scott, Mrs Thomas, Mrs Brockett, Miss Miller, Lieutenant C. J. Laws. Ensign J.M. Burnup, Richard Cail Esq., Major Potter, H.H. Brown Esq., Newcastle, E.A. Phillips Esq., Newcastle, W. G. Woods Esq., Newcastle, Cecil Hoyle Esq., Denton Hall, L. Phillips Esq., Newcastle, Captain Thompson, Captain Swan, Lieutenant Lamitee, Ensign Cook, Ensign Jobling, Ensign Crawford.

A ceremony-cum-social-evening for the testimonial of Colour Sergeant William Anderson of the permanent staff of the Northumberland Light Infantry Militia, who had been instructing the Morpeth Rifle Volunteers, took place on Friday 7 January 1861 in the Drill Room of the corps: 'Captain Brumell, the officer commanding, gave him a purse of gold and silver and elegant walking-cane mounted with silver and ivory bearing the Borough arms and an inscription'. The corps afterwards marched to St James's Schoolroom, at the Rector's invitation, where upwards of 150 of the principal inhabitants of the borough were assembled and dancing led off by Captain Brumell and Lady Elizabeth Grey, which was kept up until after midnight. The music consisted of the String-Band associated with corps under the leadership of Band Sergeant Flint

The money for this type of event would no doubt have come from the members' annual subscription, which in Morpeth's case was 10s (50p), and no doubt subsidised by the commanding officer. The uniform of the corps cost £1 14s (£1.70), a fairly basic type, but that of the officers probably cost much more.

Instances of social activity took place in Newcastle on 15 February 1861, when the Rifle Volunteers held a ball in the Assembly Rooms on Westgate Road, where 500 attended, including 'the elite of the town dancing to the music of the volunteer band' and at Blyth, on Saturday 5 October 1861, where a concert of vocal and instrumental music was held in the Central Hall in aid of the Third Northumberland Volunteer Artillery. At Wallsend, a fête was organised on 27 September 1861, to raise funds for band instruments and uniforms. Tynemouth (Artillery and Rifles), the first artillery volunteer unit to be formed in the country, were to have 68-pounder guns and ammunition provided at Tynemouth Castle. Alnwick (Rifles) were lucky enough to have retired Major General W. J. Brown CB as their commanding officer. Berwick (artillery and rifles), Bellingham, St John Lee, Hexham, Tynedale and Allendale (all rifles) with many of them having sections in outlying villages, were all busy raising funds.

Following a Royal Commission in 1863, government intervention in the form of capitation grants allowed financial assistance to be given to the less well-off members of the communities who wished to enlist, thus broadening the social spectrum. Full-time Regular Army Adjutants were sent to administer, and create some cohesion among the widely spread rural units in the form of Administrative Battalions, while units in the urban areas formed Consolidated Battalions. Regular Army Sergeant Drill Instructors were also hired. An account in the *Newcastle Courant*, 26 April 1861, notes the forming of an 'Administrative Battalion of the whole of the Rifle Volunteer Corps in the county of Northumberland, with the exception of those of Newcastle upon Tyne', and goes on to state that, 'Captain Northcote has been appointed to act as Adjutant to such battalion for the purpose of superintending and giving instruction and assistance to the several divisions', and that, 'on Monday evening [22nd] in the presence of Captain Northcote, the 5th or Alnwick Company, had inspection drill under the charge of Captain the Hon., Harry Grey, who assumed the command of that body'. Major General Brown had not lasted long.

The 2nd Hexham Rifle Volunteer Corps was a typical example of a unit in a rural market town. A meeting had been held on Monday 3 December 1859, to propose the formation of a volunteer corps in the town. J. M. Ridley of Walwick Hall was elected captain. On 7 March 1860, a letter was received by Earl Grey, the Lord Lieutenant:

> My Lord, With reference to your letter of the 3rd ultimo, offering for the Queen's acceptance, the service of a company of rifle volunteers at Hexham, under the Act 44, George III, c.55, I have the honour to inform you that Her Majesty has been pleased to accept the same. The corps is numbered as the second in Northumberland, and its maximum establishment will consist of one Captain, one Lieutenant, one Ensign, and one hundred men of all ranks.

8th (Walker) Corps, 1865.
(Painting by James Alexander)

This sanction was pre-empted, as the first sample uniforms purchased from a Mr Lyon and Mr J. Stafford, at £2 8s each (£2. 40p), were shown at a muster parade at Cockshaw Foundry on 1 March 1860. The uniform was of steel-grey cloth with red facings, brown belt, cartouche box and cap pouch, a zouve type cap (shako) and spun-silk white gloves. By Friday 18 March, the corps numbered 130, so it was decided that two companies should be formed. The companies were sworn in at the Court House by William Cuthbert, the High Sheriff, on 19 March. All the Northumberland Rifle Corps wore basically the same uniform of grey with red facings, but each had its individual badges and other insignia, as seen in Denis Wood's *The Fifth Fusilier's and Its Badges* (London, 1988). They operated in a similar manner, but with their own set of rules and regulations. The main emphasis was on shooting skills, drill and an active social life. To this end the Northumberland and Newcastle Rifle Association was formed in 1862, which held its annual competitions on the Rifle Range on Morpeth Common. One of these competitions was held on Thursday 14 July 1862, the annual inspection was held at Morpeth. There were eight individual companies on parade:

Hexham:	Captain Nicholson
Morpeth:	Captain Brummell
Belford:	Lieutenant Cully
Alnwick:	Ensign Brown
Bellingham:	Captain Charlton
1st Berwick:	Captain Ramsey
Lowick:	Captain the Earl of Durham
Composite:	Lieutenant Head

The commanding officer, the Earl of Tankerville, of Chillingham Castle, presented a silver bugle as a trophy for the winning company at the shooting competition which was won by the Bellingham Corps on 19 September.

A public profile was maintained by the volunteers in Newcastle by frequent parades on the Town Moor. On Good Friday, April 1861, the *Newcastle Courant* reported that the 1st Newcastle Rifle Volunteers under Lieutenant Colonel Sir John Fife, and the 1st Newcastle Artillery Volunteers under Captain Henry Allhussen, who managed his father's chemical works in Gateshead, a firm which provided the horses to pull the guns, announced that they would be exercising on the Town Moor. The riflemen assembled in the Corn Exchange, and the artillery in Grainger Street. Headed by the artillery, with the Rifles Band under Bandmaster Potts leading the Rifle Corps, they marched through enormous crowds on Newcastle's streets to the Moor:

… and on arriving at the west side of the reservoirs, an assemblage of human beings presented itself that has not been seen in Newcastle for some time… the delightful state of the weather brought out a great number of the fair portion of the community to witness the sight. A large number of gentlemen's carriages containing numerous ladies and families, were present on different parts of the ground, also a large number of gentlemen on horseback.

The Hexham Corps attended the Royal Review at Edinburgh on 7 August 1860, along with the Newcastle, Morpeth, and Percy Artillery. Major James Walters, *Volunteer Force*, (London, 1881), commented:

Then came the 1st Artillery Brigade, having in front the Edinburgh City Artillery, followed by a strong force from Tynemouth, Alnwick, Sunderland and Whitehaven. The companies were very smart from the geographical extremes – the Berwick-upon-Tweed and 1st Caithness; then came the Rifles. The third and fourth battalions of this brigade were made up of nearly 1.500 of English volunteers. stout and straight, from Northumberland, Durham, and Cumberland, who received loud welcomes where ever they were recognised – and welcome, it need scarcely be said, being made specially cordial for a Northumberland, composed. we presume, of exiled Celts in the Highland Garb.

This company was, of course, the Scottish Company from Newcastle, the forerunners of the famed Tyneside Scottish Brigade of the First World War.

The Cardwell Reforms of 1881 led to a complete reorganisation of the various rifle corps in the region. By a War Office order dated 28 My 1880, the units in the North and West Northumberland were consolidated as a single regiment named the 1st Northumberland and Berwick-upon-Tweed Rifle Volunteer Corps, with its headquarters at Alnwick, incorporating the 1st Berwick (1860), 2nd Hexham (1860), 3rd Morpeth (1860), 4th Wooler-in-Glendale (1860), (and, from 1862, Belford), 5th Alnwick (1860), 6th Bellingham (1860) and 7th Allendale (1860). Later additions were the 10th Lowick (1861), 11th St John Lee (1868) (later Sandhoe, then, from 1876, Corbridge) and the 12th Haltwhistle (1878). The recruiting area extended from Berwick in the north to Hexham in the south, then along the Tyne Valley to Haltwhistle, Bellingham and Allendale in the west. Then, in February 1883, they were retitled the 1st Volunteer Battalion, The Northumberland Fusiliers (Order of Precedence No. 83).

On industrial Tyneside the 4th, 5th and 6th companies of the 1st Northumberland Rifle Volunteers (1860), which had originated in the schoolroom of the Walker Iron and Alkali Company in December 1859, became the 8th Walker, and were attached to the 1st Tyneside Rifle Volunteers, which included three companies at North Shields. An addition was the 9th Crumlington [sic] (1861). The three companies at North Shields were later disbanded, as was the 9th, leaving only the Walker companies. More men joined from Mitchell and Company's shipyard at Low Walker, bringing the strength of the Walker corps up to 400 by September 1861. Headquarters were then transferred from Tynemouth to Walker. As with most other artisan companies, the men paid for their government grey uniforms by fortnightly instalments. In 1865, the corps expanded by another two companies from among the workers of the Walker Rolling Mills. The 8th Walker Rifle Corps was the first to have a central headquarters with a new Drill Hall, costing £950, built on what was waste land in Walker. It was opened in December 1868 with a public dinner paid for by Mr Hugh Taylor MP. By 1881 scarlet tunics with green facings had been adopted, and the corps took part in the Edinburgh Royal Review of that year. The corps was designated as the 2nd Northumberland Rifle Volunteers in 1880, then as the 2nd Northumberland Volunteer Battalion in 1881, and finally, in 1883, as the 2nd Volunteer Battalion, The Northumberland Fusiliers (Order of Precedence No. 84).

In Newcastle-upon-Tyne on 7 August 1860, 500 men of the 1st Newcastle Rifle Volunteers, paying their own expenses, assembled at the Central Station at 6.30 a.m., from where two engines and fifty carriages carried them and the Gateshead Rifles to Edinburgh to take part in the Royal Review by Queen Victoria. Such was the impression they made upon the people of Newcastle, that a letter to the editor appeared in the *Newcastle Journal* of 18 August 1860. A Newcastle lady who had obviously been to the review complimented the volunteers on their bearing, and the impact they had made on the people there:

> Few, I think, could see our Newcastle Riflemen leave our canny town for Edinburgh the other morning without being proud of them, and I should hope that there is not one lady in this town who was not proud to hear that our brave fellows were considered the most splendid corps in the field.

She went on to suggest that the ladies of Newcastle should start a fund to provide the corps with a set of colours and that she would be the first one to contribute £1. Just under three months later, on 7 November 1860, the corps, nine companies strong, assembled and marched to the Town Hall where a Mrs Headlam, on behalf of the ladies of the town, presented a silver bugle to the commanding officer. The bugle bore the inscription: 'Presented by the ladies of Newcastle to the 1st Newcastle Rifle Volunteers, November 4th 1860.' This bugle was kept in the officers' mess in St George's Drill Hall, opened in 1883, until the reduction of the Territorial Army in 1967, and it now lies in the Civic Centre, Newcastle, a link with a past of over 140 years ago. As with the other volunteer corps, it went through various changes of title, being designated as the 1st Newcastle-upon-Tyne Volunteer Battalion in July 1881, and then renamed as the 3rd Volunteer Battalion, The Northumberland Fusiliers in February 1883 (Order of Precedence No.213).

Above left: *Sergeant Major Cornelius Maune, 1st Newcastle Rifle Volunteers, c.1874. (Painting by James Alexander)*

Above right: *Cornelius Maune just before he became S.M. of 1st Newcastle Rifle Volunteers. The painting shows him wearing Newcastle insignia. (T. Hewitson)*

The 1st Newcastle was not always a well-disciplined and efficient unit. In 1871, seven members of the corps, four of them NCOs, were dismissed because of insubordination. There must have been some underlying friction among the companies because all the officers and men of No.13 Company left the corps and joined the Newcastle Artillery Volunteers. By 1873 the uniform had been changed from the grey, with black braiding – although No.12 (Guards) Company, all over 6ft, had touches of red on the collar and cuffs – to scarlet tunics with black facings and white belts. This dress was worn until the uniform of The Northumberland Fusiliers was adopted.

Local units attended the Royal Review in Queen's Park, Edinburgh again in 1881, during which torrential rain soaked them to the skin, causing them great discomfort on their journey home. Sergeant Leatheard of the Hexham corps described the rail journey from Hexham to Edinburgh, illustrating the extensive network of rail communication that existed prior to Dr Beeching's destruction of the system in the 1960s:

On Thursday 25 August 1881, with punctuality which augered well for discipline, the rank and file comprising 'A' Hexham Company assembled at their headquarters punctually at 5.30 a.m. in the morning. They were then marched to the station by way of Priestpopple, where they found the train already waiting for them, and seated in which were contingents from Haltwhistle and Allendale. The first stop was Reedsmouth, where the carriages containing the Morpeth corps were attached to the train, then called for the Bellingham men, and on to St Boswell's, where the other members of the Northumberland Corps arrived, and afterwards called at Galashields for a corps of Scottish volunteers. Tickets were collected at Glen Esh, and at Niddrick Junction the train turned on to the St Leonard's line and then disembarked at a point near to the south end of Queen's Park, formed into a quarter column and marched to the division in which they were to be included. The strength of 'A' Company was 107 all told, Canon Barker (Chaplain) being included. Then came a term of weary waiting in incessant rain, and in the midst of it Her Majesty, accompanied by a brilliant escort, drove round the divisions, bowing graciously as she passed along. At last came the march past. Slowly the men trudged through miniature streams and mud ankle deep to the parade ground, passing on the right a huge array of umbrellas on the heights at the base of Arthur's Seat and those above Margaret's Loch. Wet to the skin, shivering with cold, the Northumberland men's turn came at length, and at the east end of the grandstand there was a shout of 'Gan on the Northumberland' and a hearty cheer. The tune to which they marched past was *Blue Bonnets over the Border*. Again and again the cheering was renewed as the first company (Hexham) marched on, maintaining a line as straight as an arrow along the whole front of the grandstand. The review over, they marched to Duddingstone and took train for Hexham, arriving home at 11.30 and marched to the Market Place, gave three ringing cheers for Major Ord, Captain W. Gibson, and Lieutenants' J. P. Gibson and L. C. Lockhart, and were then dismissed.

As well as social events, shooting, drilling, reviews and field days, the Volunteers were called upon to carry out more solemn duties. A letter from Sergeant Instructor J.P. Carlton, 1st Volunteer Battalion, The Northumberland Fusiliers, appeared in the *St George's Gazette* of 30 June 1886, appealing for donations for the widow and three children of the late Sergeant Instructor Lawton, who had been left almost destitute. Lawton had served twenty-six years, twelve of them in India, and settled in Bellingham after serving for almost seven years with 'E' Bellingham Company, of the 1st Volunteer Battalion. He had been buried in Bellingham on 20 June with full military honours by men of the company under the command of Captain J.G. Dixon. It is certain that the men of the company would have given the widow a considerable sum. A further note in the *Gazette* for 31 August states that donations amounting to £11 19s 6d (£11.97p) had been received up to that date from readers.

3rd Volunteer Battalion NF, Ripon, 1907. (T. Hewitson)

Bellingham Rifle Corps had been raised by William Henry Charlton, a gentleman of independent means living near Bellingham. He was one of the founders of the Border Counties Railway which covered the West and North Northumberland. It was this railway system that had carried Sergeant Leatheard and the Hexham Company to Edinburgh for the review. In *Recollections of a Northumbrian Lady* 1815–1816 (Stocksfield, 1989), the lady in question, Barbara Charlton, wrote in her diary for 1861:

> The Volunteer movement was in full swing and William's latest toy, the Bellingham Volunteer Company, had now been in existence for a whole year, well cockered up by him on the least excuse. Every Saturday the local men belonging to it, with the gardener Hodgson foremost in the van, assembled in the pantry and after partaking of refreshment, would be carted down the drill ground in Bellingham; but having broken down two vehicles, one of which was my own nice basket pony carriage, it was represented that in future they must walk. William used to lavish food and drink on his beloved Volunteers but whiskey would have been to them a much more palatable beverage than the champagne that went down their throats.

Again, in 1863, she tells of assisting in, 'a most successful Volunteer bazaar at Bellingham', testimony to the involvement of family in volunteer affairs.

In October 1874 Lieutenant Colonel the Earl of Tankerville, the former commanding officer, was appointed as Honorary Colonel of the Regiment, and the Earl of Durham was gazetted as Lieutenant Colonel. Captain George Brummell of the Morpeth Corps became Major, as did Captain William Henry Charlton. Major Charlton was to serve until 1879, in which year the 12th Haltwhistle Corps, over seventy strong, was raised by Mr Andrew Blackett Ord, who was appointed Major. Among major events for the volunteers during the 1880s was the first annual camp of the 1st Volunteer Battalion, held at Newbiggin-by-the-Sea in 1884; they returned there in 1888, 1889, and 1890. Another occasion for the 3rd Volunteer Battalion was their first annual camp in 1884 at Whitley Bay, probably on the Rifle Range at Hartley, now the site of a caravan park. An outstanding event for the 3rd VB was the opening of their new Drill Hall at St Mary's Place, Newcastle, on 25 June 1883, when the Earl of Durham gave a dinner in the hall for 700 members of the battalion. On 20 August 1884, 100 men of the battalion mounted a guard of honour for the Prince and Princess of Wales when they visited the Drill Hall.

Large reviews were held on Newcastle Town Moor, such as that at the Royal Jubilee Exhibition on Wednesday 11 May 1887, when 6,000 volunteers paraded for His Royal Highness the Duke of Cambridge, the Commander-in-Chief of the British Army. There were frequent church parades in the various home locations and drill parades were held where the public could watch them.

Officers of the 1st Northumberland Rifle Volunteers at annual camp on the moor at Newbiggin-by-the-Sea, 1884. (T. Hewitson)

Unfortunately, on some occasions they were subjected to derision by children, youths and members of the public, and in later years the local press was not as sympathetic as it had been in the early days. Perhaps Sergeant Leatheard of the Hexham corps, summed up the ethos of the volunteers when he paid tribute to Colour Sergeant J.P. Gibson, who 'spared no efforts to make the volunteer life an attractive and pleasant one by promoting balls, suppers and other amusements'.

The Tyne and Tees Brigade consisting of the 1st Volunteer Battalion, The Northumberland Fusiliers, the 1st, 2nd and 4th Volunteer Battalions of The Durham Light Infantry, went into the first Brigade camp held at Ripon, in the West Riding of Yorkshire, on Saturday 20 May 1893. Sergeant Leatheard informs us that:

> This was the first time a Brigade camp had been held at Ripon, and on the route from the [railway] station to the camping ground the streets were adorned with bunting, and in the cathedral, bells rang in honour of the occasion, The Brigade halted and formed up in front of the Town Hall, and after one blast on the city horn by the horn blower, the mayor (Alderman Parkin) presented the Brigade Commander, Lieutenant General Sir H. M. Havelock-Allan, Bart., VC. KCB. with an illuminated address welcoming the Brigade to Ripon.

The *Newcastle Daily Chronicle*, Monday 22 May 1893, described the camp as being situated on Ripon racecourse, with over 400 white-bell tents and mess tents, canteens, entertainment tents and a hospital. The officers' mess was in the grandstand and a drawing room had been fitted out. Water had been laid on to the camp. On the Sunday a drumhead service was held and in the afternoon the various bands played and the camp was visited by hundreds of people.

With the Brigade numbering over 2,000 men, no doubt the publicans and tradesmen of Ripon would have been delighted to see them. Private John Gibson of Hexham composed a song about camp, likely to the tune of the *British Grenadiers*, from which the following extract is taken:

> *And there we meet upon the field*
> *Our comrades in the grey:*
> *From Allendale and Bellingham*
> *And marksmen true are they.*
> *From Corbridge and from Haltwhistle,*
> *Morpeth and Alnwick,*
> *From Belford and Berwick,*
> *We find good men and true.*

Cyclist section of the 1st Volunteer Battalion NF. (T Hewitson)

But the major happening in the forty years existence of the Rifle Volunteers up to 1899, as with the Northumberland (Hussar) Yeomanry, was the Boer War, and the call for volunteers for South Africa. The 3rd V Battalion reported in January 1900 that its Special Service Company was being formed. In February, the 2nd V Battalion stated that orders had been received to form a Special Service Company of two officers and seventy-five men for the regular battalion in South Africa. In the event, 20 per cent of the battalion volunteered to serve. The 1st V Battalion had already raised a company of two officers and eighty men: Hexham, twenty-four; Morpeth, ten; Belford, eight; Alnwick, eight; Bellingham, nine; Allendale, three; Berwick, six; Prudhoe, one officer and five men; Corbridge, one officer and four men; Haltwhistle two; and Sergeant Instructor Walton. One of the first to go with No.1 Volunteer Service Company was Corporal G. Middlemiss, who in civilian life was the postmaster at Glanton, in north Northumberland. He was the archetypal volunteer; having served with the Newcastle Engineers, Percy Artillery, Northumberland Hussars, and 'D' Company 1st V Battalion, The Northumberland Fusiliers. He was technically too old to go, but he must have been a persuasive person. When he returned he was too old for further service with the volunteers. Perhaps he regarded South Africa as his swan song. The Special Service men served in South Africa for one year. Each battalion raised a second company, but by 1902 there was a marked reluctance among the members to volunteer. There is a magnificent memorial at Barras Bridge, in Newcastle, to all the local servicemen who lost their lives in South Africa.

For the Newcastle Volunteers and the Imperial Yeomanry who returned from South Africa, a ceremony took place in Fenham Barracks on Saturday 10 August 1901, where they were presented with the Freedom of the City. A thanksgiving service was subsequently held in St Nicholas Cathedral, followed by a banquet. At Hexham, forty-two West Northumberland members of the 1st V Battalion attended divine service at Hexham Abbey, after which they were presented with their South African War medals. Ceremonies were held at Berwick, Alnwick and Bellingham, where the volunteers received their campaign medals.

A number of Scottish professionals and business men in Newcastle and the surrounding districts had formed a committee among themselves to recruit, organise and finance the raising and equipping of an infantry battalion, to be named The Tyneside Scottish Volunteer Battalion, for service in South African. This was no doubt due to a mixture of patriotism and nationalistic pride, influenced by the fact that both London and Liverpool had Scottish Volunteer Battalions. One thousand men had come forward and volunteered; a pipe band and brass band were recruited, and uniforms, equipment and insignia were priced. Unfortunately, the War Office expressed a preference for mounted troops, and this was not financially viable. There was also opposition from some of the commanding officers of the local volunteer units in the district, who claimed that this would affect their recruiting. In the end it was decided not to press ahead with the project. There was some compensation for the Scottish community in that the 3rd V Battalion formed a pipe band in October 1902. It lasted until the 1908 reforms, when it was quietly disbanded.

Members of the Morpeth Company of the 1st Volunteer Battalion N.F, serving in South Africa, c.1900. (T Hewitson)

Corps of Drums 2nd (VB) Northumberland Fusiliers, Ripon 1907, all wearing fusilier fur caps. (T Hewitson)

A celebrated member of the 2nd V Battalion attended the presentation of thirty-seven South African medals to members of the battalion in Walker Drill Hall on 18 November 1902. The person in question was Colonel H.F. Swan, who had retired after twenty-seven years in command of the battalion. He had served with the Walker corps from its first formation in 1859, forty-three years earlier. After accepting the post of Honorary Colonel, he was given a hallmarked silver engraved presentation sword and scabbard on behalf of all the members of the battalion.

Richard Haldane's reforms of 1908, which remodelled the Regular Army by creating an Expeditionary Force, a General Staff, and a new Territorial Force, meant that there were fundamental changes made in the organisation of the volunteer infantry battalions of Northumberland and Newcastle. The 1st V Battalion was split into two battalions, creating the 4th and 7th Battalions of the Northumberland Fusiliers (TF). The 4th Battalion was to recruit along the Tyne Valley, with headquarters in Hexham, and 7th NF (TF) was to recruit in the area stretching from Berwick-upon-Tweed to Ashington, Morpeth, and Bedlington in south-east Northumberland, with headquarters in Alnwick. The 2nd VB was renumbered as the 5th NF (TF), recruiting among the shipyards and industrial workers along the river Tyne and the suburb of Gosforth, with its headquarters in Walker. In the city of Newcastle itself, the 3rd VB was designated as the 6th (City) Battalion NF (TF). Its headquarters remained in St George's Drill Hall, in St Mary's Place, and it was to recruit within the city boundaries. These four battalions formed the Northumberland Infantry Brigade as part of the new Northumbrian Division, complete with its own artillery and supporting arms, and were to play a vital role in the war that was to come in August 1914.

FIVE

THE ARTILLERY VOLUNTEERS

The great guns roar'd, the fire flew,
It was a grand display;
The sea-gulls scream'd an flapped thor wings,
An' flew nor' far away.
The greet roond-shot went plish-for-plash
inti the tortured deep;
They myed the crabs and lobsters hop,
An' the fish cud get nee sleep.

Edward Elliot of Earsdon, 1862.

For many years the main centres for artillery units had been Berwick and Tynemouth. Units in the coastal towns were mainly employed as garrison artillery for the defence of the ports and coastline of Northumberland. Such was the importance of the North East defences in 1716, that according to the *History of Coast Artillery in the British Army* by Maurice-Jones (London, 1959), there were no less than seventy-six guns at Berwick, twenty on Holy Island and thirty at Tynemouth. As with the Rifle Volunteers, there was a good deal of interest shown in the formation of Artillery Volunteer Corps. The towns that had raised artillery units during the Napoleonic Wars once again rallied to the call to arms.

The first meeting of those advocating the formation of local Artillery Corps took place in April 1859, in the Albion Assembly Rooms in Norfolk Street, North Shields, where it was proposed to offer the services of Volunteer Rifle and Artillery Corps from the Borough of Tynemouth. By the first General Meeting held on 17 May, the number enrolled had risen to seventy, and a resolution was made that a regiment should be formed in Tynemouth. The first drill parade of the volunteers took place in the George Tavern, King Street, which was attended by about 120 members. Official sanction was not granted by the War Office until 2 August 1859, when the Artillery Company was named the 1st Northumberland Volunteer Artillery, with precedence No. one in the country, and the Rifles designated as the 1st Northumberland Rifle Volunteer Corps.

A momentous day for the gunners was 18 November 1859. They had their first inspection and first big gun practice at Tynemouth Castle under Captain Carpenter, who had been sent from Manchester for that purpose. The guns were two 12-pounders which had not been used for seventy years, so they were double-shotted and fired with a slow match. The target was placed 900 yards from the North Battery. A Rifle Range was sited in Spittal Dene, north of Tynemouth Park, and, in December 1860, the Duke of Northumberland placed Percy Square, North Shields, with two cottages, at the disposal of the 1st Northumberland Volunteers. Although the corps was only established in August 1860, by early September a band of thirty musicians, under the leadership of two men, Mr Hemy, and Mr Watson, had been formed. The *Newcastle Courant* of 7 September stated that:

> On Friday last the members of the Newcastle companies of the Northumberland Artillery Volunteers assembled at the Guildhall, and led by the band marched through the principal streets in the direction of Scotswood. The fine bearing and the elegant uniforms of the volunteers produced a favourable impression upon the spectators.

The black door was the entrance to the Percy Artillery Volunteers in Warkworth. (J. Winter)

Ashington Silver Model Band became regimental band of the Percy Artillery from 1896 to 1903, when the unit was disbanded. (W. Harriaon)

Both corps at this time were dressed in a light grey uniform trimmed with black braid, black belts and pouches with bronze-silver being used for officers, the only difference being that the artillery wore a busby, with a gun on the pouch, while the rifles wore shakos, and a bugle and crown on their ornaments. A corporal had to pay a total of £14 19s (£14.95) for his whole uniform. The uniform cost £5 2s 6d (£5.22), waist belt 7s 9d (38p), shoulder belt 16s (80p) and rifle £7 7s (£7.35). Later in 1860, the grey uniform worn by the gunners was replaced with the usual blue artillery uniform.

By 1862, the rifle corps which had raised detachments in many of the neighbouring villages had ceased to exist. Only the two Walker Rifle Corps remained, and went from strength to strength. The Artillery Corps flourished and in 1860 raised two new companies at Howden and Newcastle. Towards the end of that year these companies were detached and became the 3rd Northumberland with headquarters in Newcastle. An account in the *Newcastle Courant*, 6 July 1860, reported that the Tynemouth Corps were to use the 68-pounder guns at Tynemouth Castle and ammunition was to be provided for them. It also stated that rail fares for volunteers on duty would be charged at, '1 penny for other ranks and two pence for officers.' The newspaper also included a report, on 3 August, that the 3rd Blyth and Cowpen Artillery Volunteers were now a battery of the 3rd Northumberland Artillery Volunteers.

In 1869 a regular officer, Captain Jones of the Northumberland Artillery Militia, was appointed as Adjutant. The Northern Artillery Association was formed in 1876, and the Tynemouth Batteries took part in competitions at almost every meeting at Alnmouth, Tynemouth, and Seaham, County Durham. A new Drill Hall was constructed on a site obtained from the Duke of Northumberland. After the move into the new Drill Hall, a fifth battery was formed at Tynemouth, and a sixth at Backworth. The War Office, in one of its periodic reorganisations, amalgamated the 3rd Northumberland (Newcastle) and the 1st Durham (Sunderland), with the 1st Northumberland (Tynemouth), and took its name and precedence. This did not last long and the Tynemouth Corps again became an independent Regiment, but instead of being restored to its original first position of the Volunteer Artillery, it was placed third, and the two junior corps were placed before it. This caused a furore within the corps and the Borough, so much so that after a public meeting on 3 August 1880, a petition was sent to the Secretary of State for War protesting against the decision. Not satisfied with the third position, and unable to regain its position as the senior artillery corps in the land, the corps elected to be known as the Tynemouth Artillery Volunteers. They appeared as such in the Army List for August 1881, and in 1889 (Army Order 443) the title Western Division, Royal Artillery, was added. Annual camps of the Tynemouth Artillery were held at Newbiggin-by-the-Sea in 1882 and 1883. Newbiggin was to become a popular venue for volunteer camps. In 1908 the Tynemouth transferred to the Territorial Force as the Tynemouth Garrison Artillery.

In Newcastle the Lord Lieutenant sanctioned the formation of the first of the batteries in the spring of 1860, under Captain John Ismay, which very soon reached a strength of 180. It was part of the 1st Northumberland Volunteer Artillery, raised at Tynemouth by Captain Addison Potter. Another Artillery Corps was formed by Henry Allhusen, manager of the Allhusen Chemical Works on the river Tyne, who had previously served in the Northumberland Artillery Militia. The corps was sanctioned on 11 May 1860, and Allhusen was elected as Captain Commandant. At its first inception he had only two batteries to command, but these were gradually augmented until, in 1863, the now Major Allhusen had a brigade of six batteries under his command. A battery was raised at Newburn, in the Tyne Valley, in 1865 by Mr J.W. Spencer, who was commissioned as a captain, but after about six months he resigned and the battery was disbanded. Mr William Boyd, one of the partners in the Spring Gardens Engine Works, added another battery in which he was commissioned as a Lieutenant. Because of these two batteries being raised, batteries had to be reduced at Gateshead so that the corps still remained with six batteries. In July 1872 two batteries were formed at Hebburn, on the river Tyne, known then as

'Little Ireland'. The nucleus of the corps came from the works of C. Tennant and Co., and from the Tharsis Copper Works. This raised the strength of the corps to eight batteries.

In 1874, the 3rd Durham Artillery Volunteers at South Shields were attached as an economy measure to share an Adjutant. As with most other units at this period, there was great difficulty in finding suitable places for drill purposes. Shops, private houses, the barracks and even the Town Hall were utilised. Around 1863 a small hall was built at the Soapery Works, Hawk's Lane, for the Gateshead contingent. In 1870 a large Drill Hall was built near Park House, in which three batteries still had their headquarters in 1887. A substantial Drill Hall with a large parade ground was built at Hebburn at the expense of C. Tennant & Co. It was reputed at the time to be the finest Drill Hall in the north of England. Another Drill Hall, Cambridge Hall, was built in 1880 on the then Bath Road for the Newcastle Batteries. Now demolished, the site is occupied by the Brady Court building, next to St James' church on the renamed Northumberland Road.

The guns first used by the corps were muzzle-loading 18- and 24-pounders. These were replaced by heavier brass guns and a battery of 6-pounder field pieces purchased by Colonel Allhusen himself. These guns were later sold and the government guns returned to ordnance. Two 40-pounder rifled breech-loaders on travelling carriages, complete with ammunition wagons, were issued by the War Office. For some years the 40-pounders of the 1st Newcastle were fully horsed by the Newcastle Chemical Works, and were a familiar sight on the streets of Newcastle and at all the field days in the district. The expense of the horses became too much for the unit to bear so they had to be dispensed with. Gun practice was carried out at Tynemouth Castle. Colonel Allhusen died in September 1871 and was buried in Elswick Cemetery with full military honours. A report of the funeral appeared in the *Newcastle Daily Chronicle* on 8 September 1871, and it gives a vivid description of that sombre ceremony and the esteem in which Colonel Allhusen was held by the local populace and those involved in the volunteer movement. The funeral cortege was led by the 40-strong band of the corps under Bandmaster J.M. Amers and the men of the corps. His coffin was carried on a gun carriage escorted by six pall bearers, all of whom had detachments from their own units in the procession: Lieutenant Colonel A. Potter, 1st Northumberland Volunteer Artillery; Lieutenant Colonel C.N. Palmer, 1st Durham Engineer Volunteers; Lieutenant Colonel G.H.L. Hawks, 3rd Durham Rifle Volunteers; Colonel J.G. Echalaz, 1st Newcastle Rifle Volunteers; Colonel E.M. Perkins, 1st Durham Rifle Volunteers; Senor Figuerido, Portugese Consul at Newcastle. The route from his home, Park House, Gateshead, was lined by thousands of people, and the High-Level Bridge was crowded from end to end. Minute bells were rung from St Mary's and St James in Gateshead, and St Nicholas in Newcastle. He had died on 7 September at the ripe old age of thirty-five years. But in the short period that he commanded the unit it had become what was reckoned to be the best trained, and most efficient Volunteer Artillery Brigade nationwide.

Some units which had been formed during the French Revolutionary and Napoleonic Wars had managed to survive after Napoleon's defeat and the general disbanding of 1815, by forming themselves into clubs. Among them was the artillery troop of the former Percy Tenantry Volunteers, raised by the Duke of Northumberland in 1805. Former members of the troop who had been retained as the duke's personal artillery were among those keen to offer their services in 1859. There were still enough of them left after forty-four years to request that the corps be reformed. A letter was sent to the duke on 31 December 1859:

> We, the undersigned members of your Grace's Percy Corps of Artillery, would be very glad to form a Percy Company of Artillery of the Northumberland Volunteers, if his Grace approves of it, and it appears that in Maritime Districts the Government would rather see the forming of Artillery rather than Rifle Corps.
>
> That Alnwick would furnish the latter there would be no doubt; but we would like, if his Grace approved, to be the Percy Artillery Company of the Northumberland Volunteers. We have the honour to be your Grace's obedient and humble servants.
>
> (Signed)   James Bowmaker
>
> Thomas Robertson
>
> John Richardson
>
> John Henderson
>
> John Ross
>
> Nixon Stratford
>
> Robert Snowdon

The duke gave his consent, and by 9 January 1860, thirty-one men had enrolled. The members noted that the Tynemouth Artillery practiced on the sands north of Tynemouth Castle, and they proposed to do so on the sands near Alnmouth, south of Alnwick. They also agreed that

> ... all the members will find their own clothing and accoutrements and would prefer to form themselves into a committee to manage their own affairs exclusive of any other corps, owing to the drill being different, and would be more independent as to the times of practice.

They received official sanction from Earl Grey, the Lord Lieutenant of Northumberland, on 20 February 1860, under the Act 44 Geo. III, c. 54: 'The corps to be numbered as the 3rd in the County of Northumberland,

and its maximum establishment will consist of 1 Captain, 1 Lieutenant, 1 2nd Lieutenant, 80 men of all ranks.' Colonel Forster of Warkworth was requested to act as Commanding Officer, with William Dixon, a banker, being selected as treasurer. A field opposite the Infirmary was selected for drill purposes and a shed for stores was erected. The corps began functioning from 20 February 1860, and an order of 19 March fixed drill hours at 3 and 7 p.m. daily (Sundays excepted). A further order on 2 April contained the following: 'The corps will be considered as the 2nd Northumberland Artillery Volunteers or Percy Artillery Corps henceforward, in accordance with orders received from the Secretary at War.' Another article, in the *Alnwick Journal*, 15 May 1860, describes the very handsome uniform which the corps had taken into wear: 'a dark blue tunic and trousers with black braid, scarlet collars and cuffs, and a scarlet stripe down the trousers, which gave a very soldier like appearance to the men.' News of the arrival of a 32-pounder gun for the corps was announced in the *Alnwick Mercury*, 2 April 1860. It was taken to the drill ground until the battery at Alnmouth would be ready.

Every opportunity to turn out and put on a show was taken up with enthusiasm. One occasion was the arrival in Alnwick at 1.30 p.m. on 27 July 1860 of the Duke and Duchess of Northumberland. The bells of St Michael's and St Paul's pealed a welcome, and the gunners were there to fire a 19-gun salute. Stopping his carriage, the duke had a few words with Colonel Forster. According to the *Alnwick Mercury*, 'a vast concourse of ladies and gentlemen numbering nearly one thousand, not withstanding the weather, were on the grounds, attracted at once by the operations of the young soldiers.' An extensive account of the opening of the new battery at Alnmouth, which had been constructed at the duke's expense, appeared in the *Newcastle Courant*, 5 April 1861:

Easter Tuesday, 2 April, was fixed upon for the inauguration ceremony. The Battery is about half a mile east of the village. It has a stone platform and earthwork embrasures, is surrounded by a high and strong pallisading, and has two 32 pounder guns placed in position. About noon, a detachment of artillery left Alnwick Castle with two mounted field pieces, under command of a non-commissioned officer, en-route for Alnmouth. About one o'clock, the bugles of both artillery and rifles were sounding in all directions for the mustering of the two corps and bustle and animation pervaded the whole town. They marched to the station preceded by their respective bands accompanied by a large assemblage of the inhabitants. The artillery were under the command of Colonel Forster, the rifles under the command of Lieutenant Wilson. A special train had been provided for the men and their friends and the carriages were completely filled. In their arrival at Bilton, where crowds of people from the neighbouring hamlets were in waiting, they were joined by the detachment with the field guns. The corps were instantly formed, and again preceded by their bands and the mounted guns proceeded to the Battery. The field guns were not taken into the Battery, but placed on an esplanade a little to its rear, and manned by detachments. The remainder of the artillery men were marched inside where they formed line, with the two bands on either flank. After the usual military formalities the Union Jack was hoisted on the flag staff, the men presenting arms, and the bands playing the National Anthem. Immediately after this the royal salute of 21 guns was fired by the field pieces, on concluding which the men were put through the big gun exercise, at which they continued for a short time with the guns in the Battery.

On the conclusion of the exercise the artillery men were marched to the New Boat House, where a substantial repast had been provided by the liberality of the officers. The village of Alnmouth had quite a gay appearance, and was kept in a constant state of commotion by the Alnwick Juvenile Fife and Drum Band in their neat uniforms parading the streets in the afternoon and playing military airs. We fancy that Alnmouth, usually so dull and dreary, presented a gayer appearance than it has done for many a year.

By the end of November 1864, the corps consisted of six batteries recruited from the rural areas around Alnwick: Longhoughton, Felton, Shilbottle, Rennington and Warkworth. These batteries were always in a state of flux with constantly changing locations. Following the death of Algernon, 4th Duke of Northumberland, on 12 February 1865, his remains lay in state on Monday 20th and Tuesday 21st at Alnwick Castle. The corps mounted a guard of honour each day. On the 22nd the whole corps paraded and provided a funeral party from No.1 and No.2 Batteries for the procession to the railway station. The fields guns fired 72 minute guns as the party moved off. His Grace George, 5th Duke of Northumberland, was appointed Honorary Colonel of the Brigade.

Two detachments from Headquarter Batteries were sent to Shoeburyness in 1882 under Sergeant Major Watson and Sergeant Major Gibson. The joint detachment under SM Watson won the Challenge Cup given by the Corporation of London, and SM Gibson's won the Lords and Commons Prize, and the Canada Album – a magnificent album of superb photographs of Canada at the period, bound with covers inlaid with Maples leaves, contained in a velvet lined wooden case. This album was later presented to the Countess Percy and still held in the castle. Having made the highest aggregate score in all the competitions, they won Her Majesty the Queen's Prize of ten silver cups, an example of which is also held in the castle with a group photograph of the two detachments. In 1884 Battery Sergeant Major Watson was selected for the detachment being sent to Canada in July by the National Artillery Association, and in the same year a guard of honour of 3 officers and 102 of all ranks was furnished for the Prince of Wales' visit to Cragside, near Rothbury, the home of Sir William Armstrong, the world-famous arms manufacturer.

Another royal duty was carried out on 5 November 1888, for the visit of Princess Louise to the castle. New Drill Halls were built and paid for by the duke at Boulmer in 1886, and headquarters in Alnwick in 1887/88. Land for a gunnery range and a camp was lent by Major-General Sir William Crossman at Goswick, on the coast near Berwick, in 1890. In 1893 the War Office approved the construction of a new 64-pounder gun battery at Goswick. Equipment and three guns were sent from Holy Island and one from Alnmouth. Rothbury and Wooler Drill Stations were given up in 1896 and replaced by one in the thriving new mining village of Ashington, in south-east Northumberland, and one at Embleton near Alnwick. At Ashington the 32-pounder gun for drill purposes was positioned in the yard of Bothal School.

These changes were indicative of the fact that the Percy estates, and farming generally, would have been labour intensive. The introduction of agricultural mechanisation and the fluctuations of the annual hiring of farm workers, combined with the movement of labour to the new expanding coal-mining areas and industrial Tyneside, would have had a negative effect on the strength of the various batteries and potential for future recruitment. Annual camp was held at Berwick from 28 July to 11 August 1900. For the first time in the history of the volunteer movement, all ranks received pay and allowances at army rates. It was proposed in 1901 that the smaller drill stations should be closed and the corps concentrated into the three principal stations: those of Alnwick, Amble and Ashington. From 17 January the designation of the corps was changed in the *London Gazette* to that of the 2nd Northumberland (Percy) Royal Garrison Artillery Volunteers. New regulations for garrison artillery caused many of the men to leave the corps and, as the unit always had recruiting problems, particularly in recruiting officers, as well as suffering from a lack of horses and facilities for driver training, the Percy Artillery was finally disbanded on 31 October 1902.

The 1st Berwick-on-Tweed Artillery Volunteer Corps was authorised on 3 February 1869, precedence No.39. In many ways this was a unique corps. It always had just two batteries, yet it was classed as a self-contained regiment and received all its orders and other notifications direct from the War Office. One of its distinctions was that it had its own special buttons: the Berwick arms, comprising a bear chained to a tree, and they wore 'Berwick-on-Tweed' embroidered on their shoulder straps. In August 1859 a meeting was held in the Town Hall to consider the raising of a corps of volunteers. It was agreed to form a battery of artillery and a company of riflemen, but the War Office wanted two batteries of artillery before a company of riflemen could be formed. By the simple process of asking who wanted to be where, enough men were found to fill the three sub-units.

After the corps was sanctioned, officers were voted for, and Major Renton of Mordington House was elected commanding officer. It was agreed that each member should pay one guinea (£1.05) annually to the funds of the corps in addition to purchasing his own uniform which would cost just under £5. This caused some problems with the working-class members of the corps but, with the aid of the officers, and backed with outside assistance, the cost of the uniforms was reduced to £1. Eventually, these costs were dispensed with altogether. Drilling began on a nightly basis and the first regular instructor was Master Gunner Lovat of the Royal Artillery, based in Leith Fort. The corps took part in the Royal Review at Edinburgh in 1860.

In 1861, four 32-pounder smooth-bore guns were shipped from Leith to Berwick. These were mounted on Fisher's Battery, the line-of-fire being across the river Tweed. Problems with ships passing across the line of fire while entering and leaving the harbour caused Fisher's Battery to be condemned in 1876, and the Berwick Corps used the same bastion as the 3rd Brigade Northern Division of the Royal Artillery. On this bastion were placed two 40-pounder breech-loaders, two 64-pounder rifled muzzle-loaders (converted), two 64-pounder rifled muzzle-loaders (built up), and four 32-pounder smooth-bored. From the elevated position, a clear range was obtained seawards to the north of the pier. The Parade, the large open space in front of Ravensdowne Barracks – now a car park – was used for ordinary drill purposes and the Corps Orderly Room was in the barracks.

The gunners did fairly well in the big gun competitions at Alnmouth in 1868 against the Percy, Tynemouth, and Newcastle Artillery Corps. Again in 1877, two detachments were sent to the North of England competitions at Alnmouth, and came back with prizes, among them second prize for the 64-pounder competition, a gun on which they had only had about half-an-hour's previous drill. Detachments went to the national competitions at Shoeburyness, where they gained a prize for the 40-pounder gun. They were prize winners at Seaham Harbour, and in 1883 and 1884 they took prizes for the 64-pounder competitions at Irvine and Barry, at the Scottish National Artillery Camp. After the 2nd, Percy established annual camps at Alnmouth, the 'bear button' men were always invited to attend. In 1886 four officers and sixty men, led by a piper, marched from Berwick, stopping overnight at Belford after fifteen miles. The next day they marched twenty-one miles to Alnmouth. Berwick men of 'G' Company, 1st Volunteer Battalion, The Northumberland Fusiliers, accompanied the Berwick gunners. It was the first route march by northern volunteers. Royal salutes were fired for Queen Victoria at Floors Castle when she was resident there, and at Berwick, where Princess Mary of Teck and the Duke of Teck opened a bazaar.

The Berwick Corps was noted for the number of its long-serving members. The officers were mainly professional and businessmen who were deeply involved in local and county politics. One such man was Thomas Darling. He served as a volunteer in the Berwick Artillery as well as other units from 1868 to 1889, when he retired as a Major. He was a partner in the brewing firm of Johnson & Darling of Berwick. His son later served in the 1st Volunteer Battalion, NF. The Honorary Chaplain of the corps, the Venerable Archdeacon George Hans Hamilton, served thirty-eight years from 1859 to 1897. Among the gunners was Quartermaster Sergeant Makin who died on 4 June 1902, having served for thirty-six years. An Army Order of 17 January 1895 shows one officer being awarded the Volunteer Decoration, and eight other ranks being awarded the Volunteer Long Service Medal for twenty years' service.

At a meeting concerning the war in South Africa, held on 20 December 1900, the commanding officer, Major A. Tower Robertson, asked if he should volunteer them for garrison duties in Great Britain or elsewhere. There was almost unanimous agreement. Over 90 of the 110 men present volunteered immediately, with 30 willing to serve in South Africa, according to the *Berwick Advertiser*. However, they were not called for. The corps in this period also had two pipers, a father and son by the name of Heckles. There was, of course, the odd bad apple among them: Brigade Orders for 18 November 1903 notified that '1158 Gunner P. White, being drunk and insubordinate in Scarborough on 1 August, as reported by the Royal Artillery Police, was dismissed the Corps.' After nearly fifty years' voluntary service, the Berwick Artillery Volunteers were finally disbanded on 31 March 1908 due to the effects of the Haldane reforms.

In line with the other Artillery and Rifle Volunteer Corps of the county, the Newcastle Artillery Volunteers offered their services for South Africa. On 4 January the government accepted the offer of a battery of 15-pounder guns, and that any member who wished to volunteer should report to the Barrack Road Drill Hall on the following Monday. Forty per cent of those who turned up were not accepted. The battery based in the Dunn Street Drill Hall, near the Elswick Works, provided 130 men. They were examined and provided with uniforms, all of which were purchased from local businesses with financial aid from the County Fund. On 1 February the 'Elswick Battery' led by their band, marched to the Town Hall where they were sworn in by the mayor.

They were led by an impressive group of officers. Major Harvey Scott, a coal owner, commanded the battery. His second-in-command Captain J.C. Wedgewood was a naval architect in Elswick Works. Two other engineers at

Top: *Band of the 1st Newcastle Royal Garrison Artillery Volunteers, c.1890, probably at Goswick, Northumberland.*
(T. Hewitson)

Above: *Officer's helmet plate of the Northumberland Artillery Militia, c.1870.*

Left: *A member of the permanent staff, 1st class Assistant Instructor of Gunnery, Charles Barret, of the 2nd Northumberland (Percy) Artillery Volunteers, c.1902.*
(Joyce Taylor)

the works were Lieutenants W.C. McCarthy and F.G.D. Johnston. Other officers were Lieutenant Wilson, Surgeon Captain Wreford and Veterinary Lieutenant W. Dotchin, also a regular officer, Captain Morris of the Royal Horse Artillery (RHA). The battery moved into Newcastle (Fenham) Barracks on 2 February to commence training. A big problem was finding 200 horses to pull the guns, and the necessary harness. Training drivers was a difficulty as most of them were inexperienced. This was solved when the battery moved to the RHA Barracks, Aldershot. The battery was provided with six Armstrong Whitworth Naval 3in Quick Firing 12-pounder guns, and six limbers each carrying twenty-four shells and cartridges, by the generosity of Lady Meux, a director of a brewing company who bore the entire cost. These guns were much superior to the standard issue of 15-pounder guns of the RHA. They were ordered from Sir W.G. Armstrong Whitworth Co. Ltd on 4 January 1900. The actual guns had been removed from a Japanese battleship which was in Elswick shipyard. They were proved on the Artillery Range at Reedsdale in March, and shipped to South Africa with a detachment from the battery in the same month.

A mounted battery of the 2nd Northumberland (Percy) Artillery Volunteers ready to move from outside Alnwick Castle. (T. Hewitson)

Before the battery left for South Africa, a farewell service was held in St Nicholas Cathedral on 9 February, and they were entertained at a dinner at the Olympia on the 26th, leaving Newcastle on the 27th. In April the battery left Aldershot for the Boer War. This was the only Volunteer Artillery Battery to serve in South Africa, and the Elswick was regarded as the most effective artillery unit engaged in the Boer War. Newcastle City Council recognised their services: 'The Council do hereby admit the officers and men of the Elswick Battery of the 1st Northumberland Volunteer Artillery to be Honorary Freemen of the City of Newcastle-upon-Tyne.' A number of decorations and awards were made to members of the battery. Major Harvey Scott was awarded the Distinguished Service Order (DSO), as was Lieutenant Bell. Lieutenants McCarthy and Johnston were Mentioned in Despatches (MID), and 2932 Sergeant T. Howarth was awarded the Distinguished Conduct Medal (DCM), according to the *London Gazette*, 27 September 1901.

After the return of the battery, they settled into the annual training routine. As with the rest of the volunteers, great changes were to take place within the regiment in 1908.

Above: *The remains of the battery at Alnmouth.*

Left: *Boer War memorial, Barras Bridge, Newcastle, showing volunteers who died in South Africa between 1900 and 1902. (J. Winter)*

SIX

THE ENGINEER VOLUNTEERS

Oh, good mornin' Mr Stevens, wi'v been workin varry hard,
Sing hurrah for the CRE;
wi'v been workin varry hard on the dinghy pontoon hard,
Sing hurrah for the CRE.

Anon.

An innovation in Newcastle was the raising of a Corps of Engineer Volunteers under the command of Captain P.G.B. Westmacott, from personnel of the Armstrong factories at Elswick. It was sanctioned on 11 September 1860 and attached to the Newcastle Rifles. In 1868, following the formation of the Durham Engineer Volunteers, it was attached to the Durham unit for the purpose of Adjutants visits and instruction. Shortly after this, Captain Westmacott resigned and Lieutenant Thompson was promoted to Captain and took command. He resigned in 1873. In 1874 the corps was increased from one to three companies and, in 1875, Major A.S. Palmer was transferred from the Jarrow Corps to the Newcastle Corps. Its popularity among the skilled craftsmen of the district was such that another two companies were formed at this time. Another imaginative move was the establishment of an ambulance section within the corps by Surgeon R.F. Cook, the first in connection with the volunteers in the north.

An amalgamation with the Durham Engineers took place in 1880, and they were named the 1st Durham (Durham and Newcastle-upon-Tyne) Corps, precedence No. 20, under command of Lieutenant Colonel Charles Mark Palmer with headquarters at Jarrow. In January 1881, with an establishment of 1,300, another change of title was made and it became the 1st Newcastle-upon-Tyne and Durham (Volunteers), Royal Engineers, thus recognising the seniority of the Newcastle Engineers over the Durham Volunteers. The seemingly large numbers of this unit can be explained by the fact that its recruiting area was based on the industries along the rivers Tyne and Wear, with their skilled engineers and artisans. The corps now comprised thirteen companies: 'A' to 'E' in Newcastle and 'F' to 'M' in Durham. In 1882 two of these companies were transferred from Hebburn and Wardley to the engineering works of Clarke & Chapman at Gateshead, the workmen having asked to be enrolled in the regiment.

The Engineers took the lead again in 1882. Due to a rebellion led by Ahmet Arabi in Egypt, previous to the fall of Tel-el-Kebir, sixteen members had enlisted in the Royal Engineers on the understanding that they would be released, if they so wished, after the campaign was over. They proceeded to Chatham for embarkation but were not called for. Again in 1885 another detachment of the corps volunteered for active service on the river Nile campaign in Egypt. The majority of both these detachments were Newcastle men. The latter detachment returned in August 1885 and were presented with their campaign medals in front of a large audience of representatives from local volunteer corps in St George's Drill Hall, Newcastle, on 6 March 1886, by Lieutenant General Sir Gerald Graham VC, KCB, under whose command they served.

From 1876 the Engineers sent around fifty officers and men annually on various courses at Chatham, Kent. By 1887 the Regiment, as it was now classed, consisted of fourteen companies: Newcastle, six; Gateshead, two; Hebburn, one; Jarrow, five; with detachments of Submarine Miners and stores at Clifford's Fort, North Shields. For the Newcastle Royal Jubilee Exhibition of 1887 on the Town Moor, the Newcastle companies constructed the spar and floating bridges across the lake in the North Gardens of the Exhibition, tand undertook the heavy work in setting up a two-gun siege battery and magazine revetted with gabions, fascines and sandbags, ready to be inspected by HRH the Duke of Cambridge during the Volunteer Review held as part of the exhibition. The Newcastle and Durham Engineer Volunteers mounted a guard of honour complete with their own band for the duke when he arrived at the Central Station at 5 p.m. on Monday 11 May. He was met by the mayor and Corporation then went on by train to Cragside, Rothbury, where he was the guest of Sir William Armstrong. After reviewing 6,000 volunteers at 4 p.m. on Wednesday 13 May, he was guest of honour at a dinner given in the banqueting hall in Jesmond Dene. From 1888 the establishment of the corps was reduced to six companies when the Durham companies formed their own corps – the 1st Durhams.

The Boer War (1899–1902), and the call for volunteers, saw the 1st Service Section of the Newcastle Engineers sworn in to serve twelve months, or the duration of the war, on 18 January 1890 and commenced soldiering at Newcastle Barracks on the 19th. They left Newcastle Central Station at 10.30 a.m. on 31 January for Chatham. The group, consisting of one officer, and twenty-five other ranks, left for South Africa on 10 March. They were a varied group of tradesmen:

Submarine miners in working dress. (J. Winter)

one sergeant farrier, one leather hose maker, one tinsmith, one blacksmith, one wheelwright, one pattern maker, one engineer and draughtsman, seven fitters, six joiners and three bricklayers. They made up a small, self-contained construction unit. Sapper J.G. Lawson, the pattern maker, did not return, nor did Sapper R.A. Wilson, and their names are commemorated on the Boer War Memorial, at Barras Bridge in Newcastle.

TYNE DIVISION ROYAL ENGINEERS (VOLUNTEERS) SUBMARINE MINERS

It was during the period of the dredging and development of the river Tyne in the 1850s that the defence of vulnerable commercial and military ports was being developed, and in 1863 defensive military engineering was undertaken by the Regular Army. But it was not until 1871 that the first dedicated Submarine Mining Company was established, when No. 4 Company of the Royal Engineers was selected for conversion. By April 1877 there were five of these companies and the possibility of this duty being taken over by volunteer units was being considered. The War Office made proposals for the formation of a submarine mining company for the defence of the Tyne. Colonel Palmer undertook a feasibility study for such a company. The War Office sanctioned it, subject to the condition that:

Colonel Palmer would find the necessary craft, etc., at his own expense, and that the men should undergo a course of training on the river Tyne, and if found qualified for this service his application to form a Volunteer Submarine Company would be granted.

He provided not only the necessary craft, but also a considerable part of the cost of the experiments. No doubt Colonel Palmer was acting in a manner that befitted someone in his position. It is also true, however, that he had considerable business interests on the Tyne to protect. Thus it may not have been an entirely altruistic patriotic gesture. Sixty men were selected from the Newcastle and Durham Corps. The company was composed of boatmen, fishermen and artisans from Palmer's works. The first training session took place in February 1884 in conjunction with a section of Royal Engineers. This company was to prove a dedicated and highly skilled unit, and was instrumental in the formation of similar companies on the rivers Severn, Clyde, Humber, Tees, Forth, Tay, Mersey, and at Falmouth, which was later manned by militiamen.

A permanent staff of twenty-six, of all ranks, was seconded from the Royal Engineers. In 1888 the unit was named the Tyne Division Royal Engineers (Volunteers) Submarine Miners, and was given an establishment of three companies consisting of 9 officers and 189 men. Headquarters was removed from Jarrow to Clifford's Fort, North Shields. The term of service was three years, and as this was a technical corps, volunteers had to have a mechanical trade. Its members had to be above the age of seventeen and below forty-nine on enlistment, 5ft 6in or more in height in their stocking feet, 33in round the chest, strong and capable of lifting heavy weights, and accustomed to boat work. At the age of fifty years, all members except officers were made to retire. The whole purpose of the corps was to set and maintain a series of high explosive mines on the river bed at the mouth of the Tyne which would be electrically fired to sink invading ships.

For dual purpose on land and sea, a single pattern of uniform was not applicable. On parade, the division wore the scarlet tunics with blue facings, white piping and shoulder cords common with all volunteer engineers, but which were distinguished by the letters SM (Submarine Miners) on the epaulettes, and the wearing of a silver grenade on the right sleeve by all NCOs and sappers returned as efficient. In 'marching order' the home service helmet was worn with leggings and white buff equipment. For walking-out, the small round forage cap was worn. Working dress for duties afloat consisted of a blue reefer jacket with white metal buttons bearing the unit title, a blue woollen jumper, navy pattern trousers, leather knee boots, and navy pattern cap with a cap tally bearing the title 'Submarine Miners'. The officers wore the same pattern as the Regular Army, except that all buttons, lace and appointments were of silver. The normal dress for officers on duties was an undress uniform of blue with a blue forage cap with a silver band and buttons.

The first annual camp of the new unit in 1888, held in the salubrious surroundings of Willington Quay Shipyard, lasted fifteen days, of which only eight were compulsory. All current orders were publicised through the *Shields Daily News* and the *Shields Gazette*. Doctors Tait and Brown joined the division in 1889, and formed a Volunteer Ambulance Corps within the division, following the lead of the Newcastle Engineers at Tynemouth in 1875. Annual training was held in the Spanish Battery at Tynemouth, first built in 1545 and manned by Spanish mercenaries, hence the name. Annual camps for the next ten years were held in and around the area of the river Tyne. While not among the best in drill and marching exercises, the division was recognised as one of the most efficient in the country among the Submarine Mining units, regular or volunteer. This was demonstrated in 1891 when a detachment was formed among the fishermen of Cullercoats, along the coast from Tynemouth. Because they were not adept at drill and military skills, it was decided not to issue them with the scarlet dress uniforms, nor were they given weapons. However, there was no fault to be found with their boating skills and seamanship, and they were instrumental in beating the Clyde Division to a silver challenge trophy in 1893. The division's history relates an incident when a senior officer was inspecting the work of the unit afloat, and he criticised a fisherman over the manner in which he was carrying out a technical task involving the laying of a mine. The fisherman listened, then said, 'Ye stand aside Mister Souldier, an' let's me git on wi' the worrk'. The local people were involved in many ways with the division, which they sometimes referred to as either the 'Deep Sea Pitmen', 'The Fish Quay Lancers', or the 'Mussel Shifters'.

By 1879 the first searchlight had been installed at Clifford's Fort as part of the Tyne defences. The use of searchlights for coastal defence had been trialled for some years, and were manned by the Coast Battalion of the Royal Engineers. The RE Section at Tynemouth was increased to thirty-five other ranks. In 1897 the searchlight was moved from the Fort to the Spanish Battery and another light was installed in the castle. It was decided to raise units among the volunteers to man these searchlights. The Tyne Division had a number of men who were qualified, and the general intelligence and education of all ranks was above average. A new unit had been formed in 1897 from specialist electrical engineers and scientists in London to man and maintain the searchlights and their equipment on the Thames defences.

A band had been formed in 1890 under the leadership of Bandmaster N.A. Patterson, consisting of twenty-four musicians, later supplemented by a bugle band. In 1902 a small pipe band was formed but this was not a success, and all except Sergeant Piper J. Wilson of Shiremoor were discharged. His son enlisted in 1904 and the unit continued for many years with two pipers using Highland pipes. A special pattern uniform being approved by the War Office, the tartan adopted was that of the Clan Fergussen. The idea of pipers may have been sparked by the Berwick Artillery Volunteers who also had pipers. The two Wilsons served during the First World War. The father served as Pipe Major of the Tyneside Irish Brigade, using the Irish pipes, the son as Pipe Major of the 1st Tyneside Scottish (20th Battalion, The Northumberland Fusiliers) and was awarded the Military Medal for his gallantry on the 1 July 1916 on the Somme.

Piper L/Cpl J. Wilson with a drummer and a trumpeter (note arm badges), Gosport 1906. Wilson was Pipe Major of the 1st Tyneside Scottish 1914–1918 being awarded the MM on 1 July 1916. (J. Winter)

*First pattern badge of
submarine miners, c.1900.
(J. Winter)*

Annual camp for 1900 was held at North Shields where the miners took part
in defence exercises, operating the searchlights in conjunction with men of the
Coastal Defence Battalion RE. By 1902 the number of searchlights had been
increased to four, to cover a larger area of the river mouth. Changes were made
in the establishment of the unit which was increased to seven companies, 'A' to
'G', with 30 officers and 457 other ranks. The personnel were recruited from all
over Tyneside, although it is noted that only eighty came from Newcastle itself.
On the other hand, the officers came mainly from the city. Consequently, a
house was rented in Wentworth Place, in the city, where theoretical instruction
was given. Over the following years the training became concentrated on the
operation of the searchlights.

King Edward VII visited Newcastle to open the Royal Victoria Infirmary in
July 1906, and the miners assisted in the route-lining. The bulk of the troops
wore khaki uniforms but the scarlet uniforms of the Submarine Miners attracted
a great deal of attention. During this period, the War Office was involved in

closing down the submarine mining service. The bulk of the mining stores at Clifford's Fort were sold by public auction, and all the boats were sold off. One was bought by the Tyne Pilot Authority and two ended up with the Tyne Improvement Commission. The government abolished the whole system of submarine mining in the United Kingdom. Finally, on 1 June 1907 the unit discontinued its function and was renamed The Tyne Division, Royal Engineers (Volunteers) Electrical Engineers, entering a new era.

SEVEN

THE TERRITORIAL FORCE 1908–1918

I don't want to join the army, I don't want to go to war,
I'd rather hang around Piccadilly underground,
Living on the earnings of a high born lady.

Anon.

The Boer War, which had uncovered many faults in the structure and command of the British Army, was the catalyst for structural changes in the military system within the United Kingdom. The determination of the German Kaiser to challenge the supremacy of the Royal Navy in the world's seaways was being confounded by the construction of a new class of warship, the Dreadnought, and the formation of the Royal Naval Volunteer Reserve and the Royal Marine Volunteers in 1903. Enormous conscript armies were being built up in European countries, and Germany was bent upon becoming the most powerful nation in the world. It was the competition between France and Germany that was causing many politicians and far-sighted military leaders to look at the state of Great Britain and its future role in responding to potential major conflict in mainland Europe. One of these far-sighted military leaders was Major General Thomas Bigge, a supporter of the National Service League. In a letter to the editor of the *Herts Advertiser and St Alban's Times*, on 15 March 1911, he wrote:

As one of the oldest members of the National Service League permit me to appeal to those of your readers who have an hour to spare on the 22nd inst., to attend and hear the arguments which will be used and the 'facts' which will be laid before the meeting which will be held in the Drill Hall in St Alban's in support of the most important subject of the day, the absolute necessity for universal military training, if in these days of a 'world in arms' we are able to preserve the independence of the Islands and the existence of the Empire which has been handed down to us by the valour and self-sacrifice of our forefathers. We are constantly told by our politicians that this question is not 'understood by the people' but if the electorate could be brought plainly to see the danger in which our country stands at the present moment, the principles of the above League would be instantly adopted, and we should awake to realities and at last comprehend this bed-rock fact, that a nation cannot be saved by its money-bags, but by true and well tempered steel. It is simply amazing that in all these years during which the greatest land military power has been relentlessly preparing to challenge our naval supremacy, the people have failed to understand that nations however friendly, or the reverse, are impelled to certain courses by the necessities of their situation and of the power to survive. The Germans, as has so often been insisted on, are increasing their population at the rate of 1,200,000 per annum. They stand a good chance of being, so to say, 'hide bound' without power of territorial expansion. They do not possess a colony of importance, and we, ungrateful that we are, rule over the fairest portion of the earth's surface. Is it even now, at the eleventh hour, impossible to make our people comprehend that with the ever increasing struggle for the world's markets and points of vantage, it will be but a short time before an European Power so situated which can place four million admirable trained soldiers in the field, and possessing of a fleet which is rapidly approaching ours in size and efficiency, will not hesitate, if the opportunity occurs, to attempt the disruption of the British Empire, which enjoys all that they must obtain if they are to perpetuate their own development which is the most extraordinary of the age. Those who attend the meeting will doubtless do much to persuade them that the time has come to move, and with no uncertain steps; that if our Government cannot be forced to act, 1914 will see us with, possibly, but a very small superiority in those vessels, the super-Dreadnoughts, which will alone in the immediate future be able to act in the first line of a great naval engagement, and that the Territorial Forces which have been in course of formation for the past three years are over 40,000 men and nearly 2,000 officers below strength, manifestly much under trained both in drill and rifle practice, and that there seems little hope of increased recruitment which would bring these forces up to even the utterly insufficient strength of 315,000.

As a result of the changes, the office of Commander-in-Chief of the British Army was abolished, and the Army Council, which would prepare for war in peace-time, and in wartime would plan and control the command and direction of the field forces, came into being on 1 February 1904. But where would the reinforcements come from and who would provide the home defences in the event of war?

So another commission was formed under the Duke of Norfolk to report on the state of the auxiliary forces. The report was published in October 1904. This report was in favour of universal training (conscription) for national defence, and proposed the reorganisation of the existing Volunteer Force to be integrated as a well-armed and well-trained force along the lines of the Regular Army, which would then be organised into Divisions and Brigades financed by the government and capable of meeting and resisting invasion by foreign armies. It was the appointment of Mr Richard Burdon Haldane as Secretary of State for War (1905–1912), following the election of a Liberal Government in November 1905 committed to economies in the armed forces and aware of public opposition to conscription, which was to bring many of the changes advocated by the Norfolk Commission. Haldane incorporated many ideas, such as the Army Council and General Staff, from the findings of the Esher enquiry and the observations of former war ministers. The Volunteer Force was seen by many forward-looking politicians and eminent soldiers as totally unsuited to modern military practices. Until 1900 the volunteers had never been part of the Regular Army. The volunteer artillery was equipped with obsolete guns and there was no cohesive training policy. Even though individual volunteers had proved themselves in South Africa, as a formed body it would be ineffective against a well-trained invasion force equipped with modern weapons. The outcome of the various reviews and commissions was the enacting of the Act on 2 August 1907:

> 7 Edward VII C 9 (The Territorial and Reserve Forces Act, to provide for the reorganisation of HM Military Forces and for that purpose to authorise the establishment of County Associations for raising and maintaining a Territorial Force; and for amending the Acts relating to the Reserve Forces.)

These County Associations were formed almost immediately. On its inception in January 1908, the Territorial Force Association of the County of Northumberland was as follows:

The President: The Lord Lieutenant, Henry, 7th Duke of Northumberland.
The Chairman appointed by the Army Council: Lord Allendale.
The Vice-Chairman, ditto: Sir Francis Blake.
Fourteen Military Members appointed by the Army Council as representatives of the Territorial Force of the late Yeomanry and Volunteer Forces of the County.
Four representatives of the County Council of Northumberland, the City Council of Newcastle-upon-Tyne, the Borough Council of Tynemouth and the University of Durham.
Nine co-opted members representing Coal Owners, Engineers, Shipbuilders, Agriculture, Coal Miners, Boiler Makers, Shipwrights, and the Amalgamated Union of Labour.

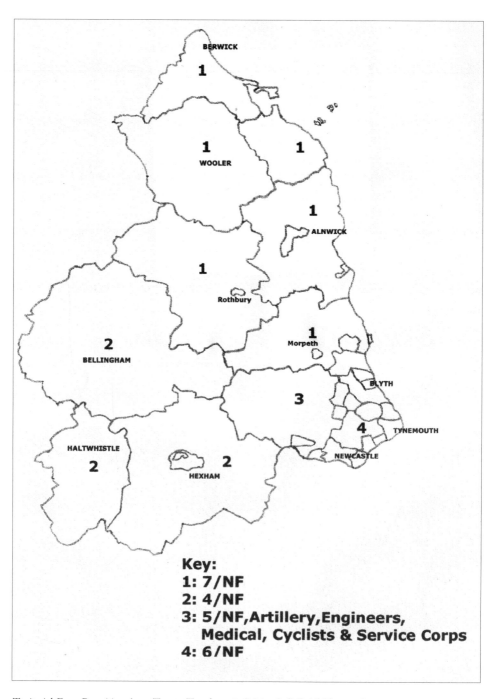

Territorial Force Recruiting Areas, Tyne to Tweed, 1908. (Major (rtd) D.M. Thornton)

Various committees were formed within the Association to administer Finance, Clothing, Equipment and Recruiting, Buildings and Ranges, Horses and Transport, Medical Services, Mobilisation, Cadets and National Reserve. All these functions were carried out by a disparate group of military and civilian members supported by a full-time staff of one Secretary, Captain A.L. Napier, first situated in the Moot Hall, Newcastle; a Chief Clerk, an ex–orderly room sergeant of the Regular Army; a Finance, Clothing and Equipment Clerk; an ex-quartermaster sergeant of the Regular Army; one typist and two office boys. When one considers the enormity of the task involved, it is amazing how well the formation and administration of the force progressed.

The financial affairs of the volunteer units had to be cleared up, plus there was the task of taking over existing Drill Halls and other volunteer property. Resolving problems as to ownership was to provide many headaches. This situation led to the appointment of a surveyor, Major M.H. Graham, a former volunteer officer. Legal problems, of which there were many, were handled by a firm of solicitors, Wilkinson & Marshall. Between the years of 1908 and 1914, new Drill Halls were built at Amble, Ashington, Haltwhistle, Hexham, Prudhoe and Whitley Bay. The Artillery Drill Hall on Barrack Road, Newcastle, was completely rebuilt and equipped with proper harness rooms, clothing stores, a riding school plus stabling for fourteen horses, and was reopened in 1911. A most important feature was the construction of a large central rifle range at Ponteland, which was partially opened in 1913 and completed in 1914.

7th NF marching to camp on Magdalene Fields, Berwick, 1909, at the first camp of TF. Note differences in uniforms and so on. (T. Hewitson)

There were also problems among the permanent staff of the new territorial units. The 6th (City) Battalion, The Northumberland Fusiliers (TF) in Newcastle, reported that a concert held in the Drill Hall on 1 April 1908 had been attended by about 700 men in uniform. During the interval, all those who wished to transfer to the new force were told they could enlist that night. Only 225 took the opportunity. Many of the older members of most volunteer corps decided to end their association with the military. Then in May it was reported that their Sergeant Instructors had lost 5s (25p) from their weekly wage due to new pay rates for the TF. Not a good start for married soldiers.

Another function of the Association was the provision of clothing to the new force. The infantry were provided with scarlet tunics with the gosling green facings of The Northumberland Fusiliers, and navy blue trousers and peaked caps as a walking-out dress. White metal buttons and insignia were worn on the uniforms as opposed to the gilding metal of the badges and buttons worn by the Regular Army. They were also issued with the 1902 pattern khaki service dress as an undress uniform for general wear on which gilding metal badges and buttons were worn. The yeomanry retained their hussar uniforms. All this took a very long time. A note in the minute book of the Clothing, Equipment and Recruiting Committee of the Association dated 15 November 1911, states that the Army Council had sanctioned gold lace and gilt ornaments for the Tyne Electrical Engineers; Northumbrian Division, Royal Engineers (TF); 1st Northumbrian Field Ambulance, Royal Army Medical Corps (TF); and 1st Northern General Hospital, Royal Army Medical Corps (TF). Another entry, dated 15 December 1911, notes that the old grey walking-out uniform of the 4th Battalion, Northumberland Fusiliers (TF) will be retained, and only those re-engaging will be issued with scarlet tunics. This was followed by a plea on 15 May 1912, from the commanding officer of 4/NF, asking for the issue of scarlet tunics to his unit.

All these changes led to a motley assortment of uniforms and civilian clothing being worn by the men at the Northumberland Infantry Brigade annual camp on Magdalene Fields, Berwick, in 1909. It was at this camp that Colour Parties from 5/NF, 6/NF, and 7/NF went to Windsor Castle, where His Majesty King Edward VII presented colours to 108 Territorial Battalions on Saturday 19 June 1909. It was not until 1922 that 4/NF received its colours on the football ground at Newburn. The reception given to the Colour Parties when they returned to Berwick on Sunday 20th was, as a 7/NF diarist records in the St George's Gazette, June 1909, 'the greatest spectacular display we have had for some years.' Lieutenant A.D. Darling, the son of Captain T. Darling of the former Berwick Volunteer Artillery, carried one of the colours for 7/NF. The ceremony was concluded by the march past of the Brigade in quarter column with the salutes being taken by the Brigadier. On the saluting base were the mayor, Sheriff and Corporation of

'B' Company 7th NF (Ashington) marching to memorial service for Edward VII, 20 May 1910. The officer leading is Captain Milburn, manager of Woodhorn Colliery. (W. Harrison)

Berwick with representatives of local civil and military institutions; all Berwick turned out to honour the occasion.

Great strides were made in the forming of the new force and recruiting became a prime objective. Certainly the smart new uniforms would have been an attraction; and the opportunity to attend annual camps with pay, in an age when annual holidays were unknown, would have been an added attraction to the men from industrialised Tyneside, in contrast to the claustrophobic underground conditions under which men worked in the coal mines of Northumberland, and the hard-worked and poorly paid labours of the agricultural workers. Two weeks at the seaside or in the lush green countryside, with reasonable food and access to entertainment would have been a wonderful break from their normal daily lives, although by the very nature of their functions the artillery and cavalry had to camp in rather more restricted circumstances.

A wholesale reorganisation of the volunteers had led to the formation of the following units within the area Tyne to Tweed, which on the outbreak of war in 1914 were:

The Northumberland Hussars Yeomanry: headquarters and three squadrons.
The 1st Northumbrian Brigade, Royal Field Artillery: three batteries and an ammunition column.
The Tynemouth Royal Garrison Artillery: six companies.
The Northumbrian Divisional Royal Engineers: two field companies, one signal company.

The Tyne Electrical Engineers, Royal Engineers: four companies.
The Northumberland Fusiliers, 4th, 5th, 6th, and 7th Battalions: eight companies each.
The Northern Cyclist Battalion: headquarters and four companies.
The Army Service Corps, the Northumberland Brigade Company.
The Royal Army Medical Corps, 1st Northumbrian Field Ambulance.
The Royal Army Medical Corps, Northumbrian Divisional Casualty Clearing Station.
The Army Veterinary Corps, The Northumbrian Divisional Veterinary Hospital.
The Army Veterinary Corps, The Northumbrian Divisional Veterinary Section.
The last two veterinary units were formed after mobilisation.

All was not sweetness and light when it came to the restructuring of the old volunteer force. A number of the commanding officers protested vehemently – the militia in particular – over their loss of autonomy. There was a great deal of friction between the British Red Cross Society and the St John Ambulance Brigade over the medical services in the county, and the introduction of a new medical service did not help. Eventually these problems were resolved by defining areas of the county to their respective spheres of activity. The 520 bed 1st Northern General Hospital, RAMC (TF), appeared in the Army Lists in July 1909, with Lieutenant Colonel W. Rutherford as commanding officer. There were twenty-seven other officers listed as available on mobilisation. Its headquarters, in July 1911, was in the Hutton Terrace Drill Hall, Newcastle. There were 109 other ranks, of whom sisty-six would be provided by the Red Cross. The nursing staff consisted of one matron, twenty-two sisters, and sixty-eight nurses.

Another new unit was The Northern Cyclist Battalion, formed primarily for coastal defence. Each man was issued with two uniforms: a service dress of khaki, and a walking-out dress of scarlet tunic with Devon or Lincoln green facings and gilding metal buttons and badges, blue trousers, blue peaked cap and white belt. In 1914 the battalion consisted of an HQ at Hutton Terrace, and four companies in Northumberland. 'E' and 'H' Companies were based at Newcastle, 'F' Company at Blyth, and 'G' Company at Whitley Bay. The other four companies were in County Durham.

As well as those units listed above, the Association became responsible for the organisation and administration of the Territorial Force Reserve, National Reserve and Cadets. Cadet corps were formed at Morpeth Grammar School, Dame Allan's School, Newcastle, Newcastle Modern School, a unit attached to the TF Company at Haltwhistle, the Newcastle Cadet Battalion, and The Church Lads Brigade of four companies. The Royal Grammar School formed a cadet corps later. These cadet units, and other independent youth organisations such as the Boy

Scouts and Girl Guides, were all part of the process of militarisation and physical regeneration of the youth of the country, which had crept into the educational and social system after the discovery of the poor physical condition of many of the young men who had been rejected on medical grounds during recruiting for the Boer War. There was alarm among the politicians and military as to what would happen if the country did go to war. The grammar schools and University Officers Training Corps were also viewed as a source of potential officers.

Right: *Member of TF RAMC, c.1913. Note the Imperial Service Badge over pocket and shoulder title: 'T RAMC Northumbrian'. (T. Hewitson)*

Below: *A platoon of 'D' Company Northern Cyclist Battalion at Lyneburn, near Cresswell, Northumberland, 1914. (J. Winter)*

A group of Northern Cyclists in walking-out dress with the Corporal in khaki service dress, 1902. (J. Winter)

Even though the new force was dedicated to the defence of the United Kingdom, it was still poorly equipped with obsolete weapons. The Regular Army has been issued with the Short Magazine Lee Enfield Rifle (SMLE) while the TF still had the old Long Lee Enfield Rifle, which the Northumberland Infantry Brigade was still using when it went to Belgium in April 1915. The Territorial Royal Field Artillery still had the 15-pounder and 5in breech-loading howitzers; the heavy batteries the 4.7in. This state of affairs, which was to continue right up to 1916, had been exacerbated by the creation of 'Kitchener's New Army' in August 1914. Virtually all the available resources were diverted to these newly formed units. An irate mother wrote a letter to the editor of the *Newcastle Daily Chronicle*, Wednesday 25 November 1914:

Sir, My son, in the 6th Battalion of the Northumberland Fusiliers, has asked me to write to you a few lines on behalf of this unfortunate battalion now billeted at the Westmoreland Road Schools. Strange as it may seem, they appear to be suffering through having responded to their country's call more promptly than others did; for the 6th NF, was formed immediately after the outbreak of the war, and the men are still without uniforms, the formation of new battalions having apparently caused them to be forgotten. It need hardly be mentioned that the men of the 6th would 'pay for the dressing' at least as well as the average man of these other battalions; for when he joined the standards of height and chest measurements had not been reduced. And yet he has to see the other men walking about in their smart uniforms 'giving the girls a treat' while he himself has nothing to show in the way of regimentals except a pair socks. These socks, bye the bye, he sometimes cannot help showing, his boots having more or less fallen to pieces after three months drilling followed by work in the trenches. Yours etc., Uniformity.

This protest was echoed by the Territorial Association, which stated that:

The disposal of the National Reserve and the enlistment into the Supernumerary Companies for the protection of vulnerable points was a very heavy addition to the other duties of the Association. They also had to be clothed and equipped and dealt with generally as other TF troops. The claims for compensation for wear of civilian clothing, prior to the issue of uniform, was also a very troublesome business. It was months before recruits received uniform and great hardship was caused. There being no arrangements for central supply of uniforms, equipment and boots, 94 Associations, let alone the War Office and the very many committees engaged in raising local battalions, were in the market at the same time competing as to price and delivery. On two occasions definite contracts for boots were made null and void owing to the War Office buyers commandeering for the New Armies the boots ordered for the TF.

'F' Company, 7th NF, mobilising outside the Jubilee Hall, Rothbury, 1914. (W. Harrison)

Royal Engineers (TF) wearing the temporary navy blue uniform until khaki could be issued. (J. Winter)

C.H. Ommanney, in his *War History of the 1st Northumbrian Brigade RFA (TF)* (Newcastle, 1927), agrees:

> Another source of trouble at this time was the clothing of the men. It had been assumed that it would be possible to lay in stocks of clothing and material after the outbreak of hostilities. This, of course, proved to be a complete fallacy, as every stitch of khaki cloth was immediately seized upon for the outfitting of the New Armies, so that before very long our unfortunate fellows were in rags. Some of those who had it wore their peace time ceremonial blue until that also went and they had no alternative but to revert to civilian clothes. Whence arose claims and much correspondence. An increase in the sick, and it is to be regretted but not wondered at, if the absentee returns, naturally from this state of affairs ... Another problem for the gunners was the supply of horses. The system was that the District Purchaser would visit about forty scattered farms and purchase three or four hundred horses and send them to collections stations at Morpeth, Rothbury, etc., all in one day – impossible – and the collecting parties arrived to no horses, no rations, and no billets. The best of the heavy horses and carts had been selected from the various stables in Newcastle. When the gunners went to collect them they had beaten to it by an officer of the Army Service Corps from Aldershot. As the owners said: 'one officer looks like another.' When they finally managed to get some horses they were picketed on Leazes Park between the Barracks and the Park railings. The water supply was the ornamental lake in the Park.

During the First World War, the strength of the TF in the county increased enormously due to the raising of duplicate units of all the pre-war territorials. The strength just before the war broke out was 230 officers and 5,948 other ranks. On 1 February 1917 it stood at 812 officers and 24,631 other ranks. As a consequence of this expansion there were sixty-four civilian clerks employed by the Association, fourteen male and fifty female, dealing with pay and allowances. Another untold story of this period concerns the camp on the Pastures at Alnwick Castle. When the success of the recruiting programme was so great that the authorities were unable to deal with the numbers attested, Lord Kitchener appealed to the Associations to help by taking entire charge of the surplus. In six days from the receipt of his telegram, the following arrangements were made:

The President (Henry, 7th Duke of Northumberland) lent a site for a hutment camp. A contract for huts for 5,000 men had been placed. Officers and nco's had been obtained to command and train the men, the entire output of the Otterburn Woollen Mills had been arranged for, a staff of tailors to make up clothing was in the process of formation; with the supply of socks, shirts, and other necessaries secured, (with the exception of boots which was always a difficulty)and preliminary arrangements for feeding had been made. On the 7th day another telegram from Lord Kitchener was received saying that it was no longer necessary for the Association to deal with this matter.

In the six years prior to August 1914, the Territorial Force had set about its new function with a commendable enthusiasm. Territorial units in the county were among the higher recruiting rates in the UK. Whether or not they were fit for their wartime role would be discovered after 4 August 1914 when the Northumberland Infantry Brigade was mobilised and the Special Service Sections were sent out to their predetermined duty stations. 6/NF notes in the September issue of the St George's Gazette that:

We received the telegram to mobilise on Tuesday evening the 4th ult., and orders were issued for the embodiment at 6 a.m. on the 5th ult. We mobilised in all respects ready for service in two hours. Five companies proceeded to Tilley's Rooms, Market Street, Newcastle, two companies to the Central Station, one To Benwell, and between the 5th and 7th ult., we concentrated in billets close to Tilley's Rooms, and on the 8th ult., the battalion marched to Forest Hall and were billeted in the neighbourhood. Between the 7th and the 14th ult., we marched to Blyth, again billeted as the garrison of the seaport, protecting the docks and the harbour until the 30th ult. On the 29th we sent a detachment of 50 men to Newbiggin-On-Sea [sic] and 16 to Amble. On the 30th ult., the battalion joined the Northumberland Infantry Brigade under General Riddell at Gosforth Park and went under canvas.

Above: *Private in the NF (TF) wearing the silver Imperial Service Badge for voluntary service overseas. (T. Hewitson)*

Right: *A Private of the Northumberland Infantry Brigade at Berwick Camp, 1909. He is wearing 1903 pattern bandolier equipment, with long Lee Enfield rifle, an outdated rifle which they still used in Belgium in 1915. (T. Hewitson)*

7/NF were at various locations along the coast, the Special Service Section at Newbiggin and the rest of the battalion at Whitley Bay. On the 15th they went to Byker and, after a short spell, moved to Gosforth Park on 18 August. Complaints about the shortages of clothing were also made by 4/NF: 'the supply of clothing and equipment has unfortunately not expanded on the same lines as the supply of recruits, but we hope shortly to be able to clothe and equip everyone', *St George's Gazette*, 22 October 1914. On the other hand, 5/NF reported that, 'between 80 and 90 men were required to bring the battalion up to war establishment. We commenced enlisting recruits at 9 a.m. on 10 August, and by 4 p.m. the same evening were up to full strength, the men fully clothed and equipped and posted to their companies'.

By September the Northumberland Infantry Brigade was concentrated in Gosforth Park with other elements of the Northumbrian Division, including the artillery, which had encountered numerous problems of their own, apart from the clothing issue. Gradually, the situation eased and the units started to become organised and settled in their new role. At the end of October the camp in Gosforth Park, which had become a quagmire, was broken up, and the various elements went into winter billets. The infantry moved to coastal defence duties, with 4/NF in the Princess Louis Road Schools, Blyth, 5/NF in Morpeth Road Schools, Blyth, 6/NF at Seaton Sluice and 7/NF at Cambois.

The gunners stayed in the park until February when they went to Larkhill on Salisbury Plain to fire practice shoots, and a sad and melancholy business it was, with rain, sleet, and no drying facilities, and mud so bad that the horse lines had to be moved every two hours. All these trials were compounded by shortages of ammunition for the shoots. They returned to Gosforth until the Northumbrian Division went to Belgium in April 1915. In Newcastle the 1st Northern General Hospital had gone straight into its designated role, and by September 1914, the unit's strength was thirty-two officers and 109 other ranks. The original provision of beds had been 540, but by 1917 this had become 2,166, and the beds occupied Armstrong College in the city, Newcastle General Hospital and a private house used as hospital accommodation. The Tyne Electrical Engineers had manned the searchlights of the coastal defences, and were busily engaged in building defensive works. The Northern Cyclists were also employed on coastal defence north of the river Wansbeck up to Bambrough.

A Territorial gun team on Melrose Terrace, Bedlington, c.1915. (W. Harrison)

All the above units formed second line units, with the infantry battalions raising two battalions each, 2nd and 3rd Battalions, for example, 2nd/5th 3rd/7th; plus the 35th and 36th Battalions: fourteen Territorial Infantry Battalions in all. By April the Brigade was based right along the coastline of south-east Northumberland. A little girl living in Cambois was not impressed by the soldierly qualities of 7/NF. In a school essay she wrote: '… the Territorials have dug trenches along the coast. When danger threatens soldiers will come to protect us…' (*St George's Gazette*, March 1915). The Brigade left Blyth for Belgium in that same month. Sergeant Jack Dorgan MM, of 7/NF, in his unpublished account of the attack on St Julien, near Ypres, on 26 April, states:

> A shell dropped among us. I found Bob Young of Ashington and Jackie Oliver of Newbiggin lying with their legs blown off. Bob Young was joking until he died and he asked me to straighten his legs and take his wife's photo from his pocket and he died with it in his hand. I sent for Jackie Oliver's brother Reddy, in another platoon. He arrived just as Jackie passed away. We had never even seen a German soldier.

Private G. Burrell DCM with his grandfather and grandmother. He was from Morpeth and awarded the DCM for St Julien, France, April 1915. (T. Hewitson)

The band of the 2nd/1st Northern Cyclist Battalion, c.1915. (T. Hewitson)

In his history, Major Ommanney writes of the attack on St Julien:

> It is now a matter of history, and most gallant history too, that the Northumberland Infantry Brigade, raw Territorials fresh from England, advanced against St Julien the following day, the 26th of April, and captured it most brilliantly, but were compelled to evacuate it. The General (Brigadier General J.F. Riddell) and hundreds of his magnificent Brigade were killed, and many others found themselves back in Newcastle, wounded, within a week of their landing in France.

Casualties within the Brigade for this action were forty-two officers and 1,912 soldiers – a terrifying introduction to industrialised warfare. This was the first territorial brigade (as such) to go into action as a brigade during the First World War. On 12 May 1915 the Northumbrian Division was renamed The 50th (Northumbrian) Division. The three infantry brigades were also renamed: the Northumberland Brigade as 149 Brigade, York & Durham Brigade as 150 Brigade, and Durham Light Infantry Brigade as 151 Brigade. All the territorial units between the Tyne and Tweed served with great distinction throughout the war.

An individual territorial of the 1914–1918 conflict who deserves a special mention was the late Colin Finch, who was described as the most decorated soldier in Gateshead. He had enlisted in 6/NF in 1909 and served with the battalion throughout the war. As a Sergeant in 1916, he was awarded the Military Medal 'For Bravery in the Field', as reported in the *London Gazette*, 11 October 1916. As a Company Sergeant Major in 1917 he was listed for the award of the Military Cross in the *London Gazette*, 18 July 1917. At that time this award was only granted to officers and warrant officers. The citation reads:

No.265297 CSM Colin Finch, Northumberland Fusiliers. He took command of the company and commenced the consolidation of the position won. On the following day, when owing to heavy hostile shelling, some men were buried, he went forward to their assistance and dug them out, in full view of the enemy.

His next and final award was the Distinguished Conduct Medal in the *London Gazette*, 3 September 1918, which reads:

No.265297 RSM Colin Finch MC. MM. For conspicuous gallantry and devotion to duty. When an ammunition dump was set on fire by enemy shelling he extinguished the flames at great personal risk. His courageous and prompt action saved a large quantity of ammunition, and prevented many casualties, as there were a large number of troops in the neighbourhood.

The *Gateshead Post*, 1 March 1973, recording his death, stated that: 'When Colin Finch was captured in 1918, Fritz [the Germans] were alleged to have told him; 'we've been looking for you for months.' On his return to Gateshead, he was given a reception by the mayor, who presented him with an engraved silver watch awarded by the council. He was obviously a very brave soldier, and an outstanding example of a 'Weekend Warrior'.

A territorial machine gun section, probably of the 4th Battalion NF (TF), c.1906.

EIGHT

THE TERRITORIAL ARMY
1920–1945

We mobilised some weeks ago,
To serve our country's call;
To punish Jerry for his tricks,
And cause old Hitler's fall.

Sergeant W. J. Dibble, 1940.

Due to extensive army reorganisation in 1918, 7/NF was transferred to the 42nd Division on 10 February as Pioneer Battalion. 4/NF, 5/NF, and 6/NF were reduced to training cadres on 4 July. This happened throughout the three infantry brigades, and the 50th (Northumbrian) Division was reorganised with new battalions. Along with the war-raised units the Territorial Force stood down at the end of the war. It was resurrected on 30 January 1920. Economic factors caused the loss of forty infantry battalions across the country. Coastal defence was to be left to the Royal Garrison Artillery and Royal Engineers. However, the reductions did not affect the Northumberland Infantry Battalions which, by June, were reporting that the recruitment rate was increasing. No doubt the appeal of two weeks' annual camp at Scarborough from 14 August was an added attraction. But the Northern Cyclist Battalion was not reformed. The former 'G' Company Drill Hall at Rockliffe Avenue, Whitley Bay, and Clifford's Fort, North Shields, were occupied by the Tyne Electrical (Fortress) Royal Engineers, with one Works Company and one Electric Light Company. This unit had been formed from the old Tyne Electric Engineers. During the First World War the Tyne Electrics had been involved in anti-aircraft defence all over the United Kingdom, with no fewer than fifteen Searchlight Companies and seventy-six Searchlight Sections overseas.

An award was authorised in April 1920 for those members of the Territorial Force and Territorial Force Nursing Service who had volunteered for service overseas on or before 30 September 1914, and who rendered such service. The medal was granted to those who: (a) were serving in the TF on 4 August 1914; or (b) had completed a period of not less than four years with the TF before 4 August 1914. It was provided that they: (i) undertook verbally or by written agreement, on or before 30 September 1914 to serve outside the United Kingdom, such agreement being operative after 4 August 1914; (ii) served outside the United Kingdom between 5 August 1914 and 11 November 1918, both dates being inclusive; and (iii) did not qualify for the award of the 1914 Star. The medal was in bronze with a straight bar suspender, and the effigy of King George V with the usual legend on the obverse. On the reverse is the inscription: 'Territorial Force War Medal Voluntary Service Overseas 1914–1919'. The ribbon was watered yellow with a green vertical stripe 4.5mm wide, an equal distance from each edge.

Above left: *Unknown trooper of 49th Royal Tank Regiment, c.1945.*

Above centre: *'Muriel', a Private in the ATS, c.1940. She is attached to the RASC. See the badge over pocket of the tunic.*

Above right: *Unknown Private, Royal Army Medical Corps, August 1941. Note the cloth slip on shoulder titles.*

(All photographs: T. Hewitson)

Ponteland Rifle Range, 1921. The huts in the background were built during 1913–1914. (T. Hewitson)

Along with the Northumberland Hussars, other units in the Tyne to Tweed area volunteered for the Defence Force raised during the National Coal Miners strike in April 1921. Stations at Blyth and the Spanish Battery, Tynemouth, were manned by the Tyne Electrics. Of the Northumberland Fusiliers Battalions, 4/NF had 'B' and 'D' Companies based in Corbridge, with 'A' and 'C' in Hexham. At Walker, 5/NF had Companies along the tyne. In Newcastle 6/NF was guarding vulnerable points in company with the Hussars. 7/NF had 'A' and 'B' Companies at Morpeth, 'C' Company at Alnwick with 'D' Company at Berwick. A Regimental Order No.136, dated 13 June 1922, concerning all battalions of The Northumberland Fusiliers, stated that, 'the title of Private will be discontinued and the title of Fusilier be substituted'. A further acknowledgement of the contribution of the Territorial Force during the First World War was the promulgation of an Act in 1922:

11/12 George V c. 37. (The Territorial Army and Militia Act. To provide for the application of a new designation ('Territorial Army') to the Territorial Force and the Special Reserve, and to repeal enactments relating to the Militia and Yeomanry.

In a rather unlikely location – Newburn Football Ground – a ceremonial event took place on 15 July 1922. For some reason 4/NF had not received colours with the rest of the Northumberland Infantry Brigade in 1908. But on that day a King's colour and Regimental colour, the gift of the ladies in the battalion recruiting area, were presented to the battalion by the Colonel of the Regiment, Major General Sir P. S. Wilkinson KCMG, CB. The King's colour was carried by Lieutenant R. Wood, and the Regimental colour by Lieutenant W.M. Gibson MC, both of whom had served with 4th Battalion during the war. Lieutenant Wood was later to command the battalion in France in 1940.

The normal training cycles, combined with the social aspects of the TA, were carried on with the same level of enthusiasm among the hardcore members. An example of the way times have changed in the industrial, social and cultural life of the North East is demonstrated in 7/NF notes, in *St George's Gazette,* 22 August (1927, p.126):

> Congratulations to the Band on their fine performance in winning the Band Contest at Morpeth Miners Picnic on 15 July. No less than 16 Bands competed. The tone and execution of the euphonium and solo cornet were much admired by the crowd. Again on 7 August the Band competed in the contest at the Morpeth Sports and secured two prizes.

The two competitions would have been won wearing their other uniform, that of Netherton Colliery Band. The entire band, under Bandmaster Moore, had been recruited in 1921 by Captain the Honourable W.J.M. Watson-Armstrong (later the second Lord Armstrong of the second succession).

In St Nicholas Cathedral, Newcastle, on 3 September 1922, attended by all the most notable military and civil representatives of the county and the city, Brigadier General the Honourable Charles Lambton DSO unveiled a memorial to Brigadier J.F. Riddell, killed at St Julien in 1915 while commanding the Northumberland Infantry Brigade. The memorial is in the form of a cartoon by Louis Raemaekers (1869–1956), a Dutch artist who had gained a worldwide reputation through his striking anti-German war cartoons. It can still be seen on the north wall of the cathedral.

Another recognition of the sterling service of the territorials in that great conflict was an order by the War Office, dated 5 July 1924, headed 'PRE-WAR BATTLE HONOURS EMBLAZONED ON COLOURS':

> In view of the decision that there will be only one Honours list for a regiment or corps, approval is now officially given for Territorial Army battalions carrying colours to emblazon on the regimental colour the pre-war battle honours of their regiment or corps, as shown in the Army List. Money grants are to be made to Territorial Associations, to enable this work to be carried out. This change will involve the removal of existing battle honour scrolls from regimental colours; the embroidering on both sides of the regimental colours a new outer wreath on which the scrolls will be placed; and the provision and fixing on regimental colours embroidered battle honour scrolls. The cost of any other alteration or repairs to colours may not be borne by Army funds or public funds of County Associations.

The 2/7th NF, was the only second line battalion of the regiment to serve overseas. It served in England until December 1917, then went to the Middle East, serving in Cairo, Khartoum and Port Said until June 1919 when it returned to the UK. On 22 April 1923 the silk Union Flag of the battalion was laid up in St James' church, Morpeth. Due to the National Strike in 1926, there were no annual camps held for the TA. Most of the units took the opportunity to hold social events for the families of the territorials, such as sports days, outings, and children parties.

During the years following the end of the Great War, the Territorial Association continued its programme of new Drill Halls in the county. Halls were built at Newburn, Amble and Morpeth in 1928. On Saturday 27 May a bugler sounded the Last Post and the flag was lowered within Clifford's Fort. After 256 years, the Fort was no longer a military station. A new Drill Hall had been built near Tynemouth Railway Station. On another occasion, on 10 October 1928, HM King George V opened the Tyne Bridge in Newcastle. Streets were lined by men of the Royal Naval Reserve (RNVR) and Northumberland TA units, with 100 men of the Tyne Electrics lining Northumberland Street.

Cookhouse 7th NF, Pwllheli 1925: 'The thicker the meat, the thicker the man'. (T. Hewitson)

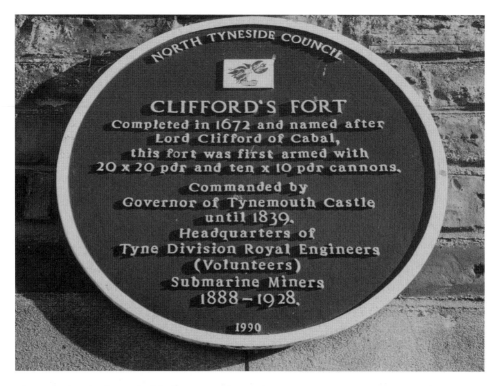

Plaque recording the closure of Clifford's Fort in 1928. (J. Winter)

Band of 4th NF (Tyne Valley Boys), annual camp, Pwllheli, Wales, 1925. (T. Hewitson)

Events that demonstrated the hazardous occupations of territorial soldiers in the industrialised areas of south-east Northumberland and Tyneside, were the frequent deaths reported in the various unit records and the local press. Sad examples were the coal miners of Woodhorn Colliery, near Ashington, who had a tradition of service as volunteers and territorials up to its closure in 1981. The author had two uncles working at the colliery who volunteered in 1914; one with the Northern Cyclist Battalion, whom in 1918 was awarded the Military Medal, and his brother, who served with the 16th (Newcastle) Battalion, The Northumberland Fusiliers. The death is recorded of ex-sergeant Walter Hughes of Ashington, medically discharged in 1916 after being gassed while serving with 7/NF. Having been back at his work for just one week, he was tragically killed in a gas explosion at Woodhorn Colliery on Sunday, 13 August 1916. Surviving one man-made war, he had died in a war against nature. He was buried with full military honours. Almost thirteen years later, on Monday 13 May 1929, Sergeant W. Kay, a serving member of 7/NF, was killed by a fall of stone. He was also given a military funeral by his comrades. Then, on Monday 7 November 1932, Sergeant T.R. Nixon of 'Y' (Haltwhistle) Company, 4/NF, living and working at nearby Lynemouth Colliery, was killed. He was attached to 7/NF, for training. Members of his company from Haltwhistle were his underbearers. In 1929, the association of the TA with the miners in the Ashington area was demonstrated when all the members of North Seaton Colliery Band, under Bandmaster Robert Lee, enlisted in 7/NF, replacing Nertherton Colliery Band.

Coal miners underground. (D. Gunn)

The funeral of Sergeant W. Kay, killed at Woodhorn Colliery, 13 May 1929. (W. Harrison)

North Seaton Colliery Band (Band of 7th NF), c.1930. (W. Harrison)

There were no annual camps in 1932, owing to the economic situation prevailing at that time. In the Army List for July 1933, the designation of the 'Electrics' is shown as:

Royal Engineers.
11(b) Electrical Engineers.
Tyne Electrical Engineers. R E.
No. 1 (E. L. & Works) Company
307th (Tyne) A.A.S.L. Company

From 1929, 307 Anti-Aircraft Searchlight Company attended annual camps on Royal Air Force (RAF) stations, mainly Manston in Kent, and also at Biggin Hill of Second World War fame.

1935 was a notable year in the territorial calendar. This was the Jubilee Year of King George V, and selected members of the TA received Jubilee medals. By a Royal Order in June 1935, The Northumberland Fusiliers were granted the Royal Prefix, 'The Regiment will henceforth be designated as The Royal Northumberland Fusiliers, and is permitted to retain its present facings [gosling green]'. This was another honour, as royal blue facings were usually worn by Royal Regiments. Annual camp for 149 Brigade in the Jubilee year was held in a tented encampment on the Pastures opposite Alnwick Castle. All four battalions of Fusiliers, with 72nd and 74th Field Brigades RA (TA) and 149 Field Ambulance RAMC (TA) were also in camp. At the end of the camp, on Friday 28 June, the entire Brigade marched out of Alnwick at 8 a.m. at the start of a route march to Newcastle. The first stop was at Felton for a meal, and they arrived at Morpeth at 5 p.m., where they were to spend the night. Saturday was a day of rest – for some. The officers of the brigade entertained the mayor, aldermen and councillors of Morpeth to lunch in the Queen's Head. The massed bands of the brigade gave a concert in the Public Gardens, and the massed corps of drums performed a Retreat Beating at 6 p.m., watched by large crowds. On Sunday 30 June, 149 Brigade and the Field Ambulance marched out of Morpeth at 8 a.m. A halt was made at Low Gosforth Park for a meal, and shortly after 2 p.m. the brigade marched onto the Duke's Moor, Gosforth, where the two mechanised Field Brigades who had motored down on Sunday were waiting for them. They were reviewed by Major General Herbert CMG, DSO. The units then returned to their respective Drill Halls.

It was not until 1937 that the government became alarmed at the situation evolving with the Nazi regime in Europe. The army's main defence priority in December 1937 was the provision of anti-aircraft defences at home. As a consequence, many TA infantry units were converted to that role. Among them was 5/RNF with its headquarters at Walker, on the Tyne. It was re-titled the 53rd Searchlight Regiment. The Tyne Electric Engineers began a series of weekend training courses at their Tynemouth Drill Hall for young officers of the battalion on their new 'weapons', the sound locator and the searchlight. The battalion was absorbed into the 30th (Northumbrian) Anti-Aircraft Group, part of the 2nd Anti-Aircraft Division, which covered the area from Leicester to the Tyne. Eventually there were five ack-ack divisions covering the United Kingdom. Because of strong opposition to the conversion, a concession to the battalion was that they were able to retain their Fusilier badges and insignia.

An unusual peace-time event took place on 26 September 1938 when Leslie Hore-Belisha, Secretary of State for War (1937–1940), signed a proclamation calling out officers and men of the anti-aircraft and coastal defence units. It was an Act unprecedented in our history. Not an army reservist had been recalled to the Regular Army, and it was not until twenty-four hours later that the Naval reserves were called forward. It is fairly obvious, in hindsight, that it was a trial of the efficiency of the mobilisation procedures and the logistical back-up they would need. A further shake-up came in November 1938. 149 Brigade was disbanded, with 4/RNF being reorganised as a motorcycle battalion. It had no counterpart in the Regular Army. In south-east Northumberland 7/RNF was to become a machine gun battalion. In Newcastle 6/RNF was converted to an armoured role as a tank battalion to be known as the 43rd Battalion (6th Battalion The Royal Northumberland Fusiliers) Royal Tank Corps. This battalion was also allowed to retain its Fusiliers badges for a short period, with the addition of a cloth tank badge sown on the right sleeve, and a black beret.

Hore-Belisha opened a campaign to double the size of the Territorial Army in March 1939. Such was the response in Northumberland and Newcastle that the second line battalions were very quickly recruited up to establishment. 4/RNF formed a duplicate battalion which was numbered 8/RNF. The 53rd Searchlight Regiment merely doubled its numbers, thus creating a unit 1,200 strong. In Newcastle the 43rd RTC duplicate was designated as the 49th RTC. 7/RNF second line battalion was numbered as the 9th Battalion RNF, and lettered its companies 'W', 'X', 'Y', 'Z', and 'HQ'. In the July 1939 notes in *St George's Gazette*, The 53rd Searchlight Regiment reported that its detachments:

> ... were located all over on a tour of duty lasting one month. Every man without exception
> being called up for one month. Headquarters remained at Walker, with one company
> headquarters camp at Birtley, County Durham, and another at Gosforth Park. Their

Signals, Northumberland Fusiliers, Ripon, 1927. (T. Hewitson)

4th RNF TA, Blandford, Dorset. (D.R. Wood)

detachments were scattered up to ten miles away. Each detachment camp consisted of three bell tents housing an NCO, nine men and various stores, with a cooking shelter and (to many of them) the unusual sanitary convenience in close proximity. Erected close by was the searchlight and its sound locator and a short distance away the electricity generating machine, either in the form of a lorry or a road trailer.

On 24 August 1939 the Regiment, as it was now termed, consisting of 408, 409 and 410 Companies, was mobilised and dispersed over a wide area of Durham and Northumberland in their ack-ack role. Following a change of designation in August 1940, Searchlight Companies became known as Batteries. November 1941 saw a new 565 Battery join the regiment, which was sited in the area of Morpeth to the north and Whitby to the south. Early in 1944 the regiment moved to the south of England, where they became part of the air defences of Portsmouth and Southampton. By January 1945 it had been converted to a Garrison Regiment titled 638 Regiment RA (RNF) (TA). After a while, all the A1 men under thirty years old were transferred to other units and the regiment was reroled as a 'B' type (Garrison) Infantry Battalion. The battalion went to Norway in June 1945 where it was involved in the disarming of the German Army and the repatriation of Russian Prisoners of War (PoW) and displaced persons (DP). The battalion was placed in suspended animation in October 1945.

53rd Searchlight Regiment RA (Late 5 NF), 'operating a 90cm searchlight'. (The TA Today, 1939)

Stalag XXc, 1940. Fusilier Purvis DCM is seated in the front row, wearing a white lanyard. (J. Charters)

Of all the units that had been involved in the wholesale reconstruction of 149 Infantry Brigade, the two RNF machine gun battalions 7th and 9th, were the unluckiest. Both battalions were to go into captivity; the 7th at St Valery, France on 12 June 1940, where virtually the whole battalion became PoWs as part of the 51st Highland Division, and the 9th taken at Singapore on 17 February 1942 with the 18th Division. In a brief period of action before capitulation, the battalion lost twenty-two killed and died of wounds. 152 died as prisoners of the Japanese. The 7th was reformed in September 1940 by the simple process of renaming 15/Durham Light Infantry as 7/RNF. This new battalion landed in Normandy with 59 Division on 29 June 1944. It took part in the heavy fighting around Caen. On 19 August 1944 the division was disbanded due to the shortage of manpower. Those divisions that had fought the hardest and suffered the heaviest casualties were chosen. The 50th (Northumbrian) Division suffered the same fate a few months later. On 26 August 7/RNF ceased to exist, and 9/RNF was never reformed after the surrender at Singapore.

In 1940 4/RNF was in France and Belgium in its motorcycle reconnaissance role, and the bulk of the battalion got away from Dunkirk, as did 8/RNF and 9/RNF who had been employed on airfield construction. The defence of Steenbecque Ridge, Belgium, saw 9/RNF distinguish themselves; a congratulatory signal from Major General H.O. Curtis, commanding 'POL Force', read: 'Well done. If you had not held Steenbecque Ridge against the tanks and infantry for 48 hours the Boches might now be in Dunkirk. The ninth have enhanced the traditions of the Fighting Fifth.'

New roles were found for 4/RNF and 8/RNF after Dunkirk. 4/RNF became the first reconnaissance battalion in an experimental role, eventually returning to the 50th (Northumbrian) Division. It sailed with the division for the Middle East on 24 June. After some months the battalion was reorganised as a motorised battalion, and by April 1942 the battalion was virtually decimated in the battle of the Cauldron, with the action at Ruweisat Ridge on 14 July its last as 4/RNF. A small cadre returned to England to reform the battalion, and the men who were left were transferred to other regiments. 8/RNF remained in the UK. In November 1940 the 8th joined the 3rd Division of which they were destined to become the Divisional Reconnaissance Regiment. Their designation was changed in the spring of 1941 to the 3rd Reconnaissance Regiment (NF). Elements of the regiment landed on 6 June 1944 (D–Day), and the rest landed on the 8th and fought through the rest of the war in North West Europe. They were not allowed to retain their Fusilier cap badge but they retained the regimental flash until they were disbanded at the end of the war.

After returning to England in December 1942, the cadre of 4/RNF was based in North Seaton Hall, near Newbiggin-by-the-Sea. Here the battalion was converted to a support role consisting of battalion headquarters and two support groups, each group having one Vickers machine gun company, one 4.2in mortar company, and one light anti-aircraft company. This figuration was changed when the unit was transferred to VIII Corps; and on 26 April 1944, 4/RNF was reorganised into three independent machine gun companies, with No.1 with the Guards Armoured Division, No2. the 11th Armoured Division, and No3. the 7th Armoured Division. All three landed in Normandy, No.3 on 8 June 1944, No.2 on 15 June, and No.1 on 25–26 June. These three companies fought right through into Germany with their respective divisions. Of the four RNF infantry battalions which had been given new roles in 1938–39, the former 6th (City) Battalion had the most peaceful war. It remained in Britain on anti-invasion duties until 1941, when it became part of the 33rd Armoured Brigade. It was going to take part in the invasion of Sicily but, at the last moment, the Brigade was replaced by a Canadian unit. The Brigade was then transferred to the 79th Division, engaged on experimental development of specialised armoured vehicles, where it remained until February 1945. It was equipped with Grant Canal Defence Light Tanks (CDL), vehicles designed to produce artificial light with searchlights – 'Montgomery's Moonlight'– and a Sherman tank. It sailed for the Far East in July 1945, arriving in India the day before the Japanese war ended. The regiment remained in India, engaged in internal defence duties. It was not until 1947 that the regiment was disbanded in India. Insult was added to injury when the unit was renumbered 2nd/43rd RTR, a new 43rd RTR (TA) having been reformed in Newcastle after the reconstitution of the Territorial Army. As with the 43rd RTR, its second line unit 49th/RTR, spent the early years of the war in experimental work with CDL tanks. The unit proceeded to France with the 1st Tank Brigade in August 1944, but was not actively engaged for some time. Towards the end of 1944, the brigade was disbanded and the 49th was converted into an Armoured Personnel Carrier Regiment using 'Kangaroos' – Sherman tanks with turrets, used to carry troops forward in an assault. The regiment took part in all the main battles from October 1944 right up to the end of hostilities in May 1945.

The Royal Army Medical Corps units were not idle. The 1st Northern General Hospital had not been reformed after the First World War, until 1936, when it was decided to expand the Territorial General Hospital Service, and it appeared in the Army List of October 1937. Recruiting began for 1st /NGH before the end of the year. By July 1939 its strength was 161, all ranks, and it was renamed 4th (1st Northern) General Hospital RAMC (TA). On 1 September 1939 the hospital was mobilised at Church Crookham, and on 16 September it left for Dieppe, France, where it maintained a Field Hospital until the withdrawal from France in June 1940. On 18 May the NGH sailed for El Kantara, Egypt, where it established a hospital which operated at that location until it was disbanded on 24 January 1946. 149 Field Ambulance served with 50th (Northumbrian) Division throughout the war, as did the TA Royal Engineer and Royal Signals units of the division.

In Newcastle the gunners had been redesignated as 72nd (Northumbrian) Brigade RFA (TF) in 1921. It was renamed again as the 72nd (Northumbrian) Field Brigade RA (TA) in 1924. Another change saw the brigade title becoming 72nd (Northumbrian) Field Regiment RA (TA). This regiment suffered severe casualties in the Western Desert in 1942 and was reduced to a cadre. The second line of the 72nd Regiment, which was raised in 1939, was redesignated as the 124th Field Regiment RA (Northumbrian) (TA) and was placed in suspended animation in 1946. The Tynemouth Royal Garrison Artillery (TF) was reformed in 1920, and renamed as the Tynemouth Coast Brigade RGA (TA) in 1921. In 1924 it became the Tynemouth Heavy Brigade RA (TA) and its headquarters moved to Blyth. In 1938 another change of title took place. The brigade became the Tynemouth Heavy Regiment RA (TA), and a reorganisation was carried out in 1940 when the regiment was divided to form 508 (Tynemouth) Coast Regiment RA (TA), 509 – with headquarters at Sunderland – and 510 (Tynemouth Coast Regiments RA (TA); 520 Regiment, with headquarters at

John (standing) and James, the Charters brothers, 7th RNF. They were taken Prisoners of War at St Valery, France, in June 1940.

Blyth, was placed in suspended animation in 1944. All very confusing, but it must have kept some people busy in headquarters somewhere!

Such was the contribution of the Territorial Army from Tyne to Tweed during 1939 to 1945. There were some strange incidents involving territorials from one territorial company of fusiliers based in a mining village in Northumberland; and three cases demonstrate dedication, sheer courage and determination. Company Sergeant Major Ted Burns had enlisted as a sixteen-year-old boy in the 2nd/7th Battalion in April 1915. He was wounded twice and gassed. Demobilised in 1919, he rejoined 7/NF in 1922. He was a postman in his civil life but was a dedicated territorial soldier. Taken prisoner with the rest of the battalion at St Valery in June 1940, he was not released until 1945. He had two unfortunate wars but at least he survived. After the war, he was an enthusiastic member of the local Comrades Association until his death. He epitomised the spirit of the territorials. There were also the two Charter brothers who were also taken at St Valery. One of their company, who managed to escape from France, visited their home in England and told their father and mother that he had seen them both dead. As they had not received any notification from the authorities, the family were naturally extremely upset. However, while they were being marched into captivity, John, the eldest brother, managed to pass a message with their names and home address to a French lady. She managed to get a letter to the Red Cross in Switzerland who notified the family, enclosing the French woman's letter. They took it to the headmaster of a local school who translated it for them. It was not until much later that the family received official notification that they were alive and Prisoners of War. Another member of the same company was the only fusilier of the regiment to be awarded the Distinguished Conduct Medal for a successful escape from a prison camp. The citation in the *London Gazette*, 26 July 1945, for the award, reads:

4270748 Fusilier Joseph Purvis 7/RNF

Following his capture at St Valery-en-Caux on 12 June 1940, Purvis was transferred to Germany, where he was imprisoned at Stalag XXc, Stalag XIc and subsidiary working camps. When employed in the salt mines at Volenkenroda during September 1941, he made his first attempt to escape; with one companion he emerged from a mine shaft, collected their hidden store of food from the baths, climbed through a window and over the fence. Although after three days his companion was compelled to give himself up, Purvis continued alone towards to Switzerland. On the tenth day of his solitary journey he was discovered by a hunting party and handed over to the authorities. Transferred to Merkers in December 1942 he participated in a mass breakout but was recaptured within forty-eight hours. At the beginning of February 1943 he planned an escape with another person employed nearby. On 29 April the details were complete, and while two other prisoners attracted the guard's attention Purvis climbed the twelve foot fence. In anticipation of being joined by his companion, he remained in the locality for three days. But on 2 May he hid in a railway wagon and covered himself with salt. Half an hour later the wagon was sealed. After travelling thus for no less than five days Purvis heard both French and German spoken, and getting out he found that he had reached Switzerland. For fourteen months he remained there before he was evacuated to France. When the arrangements for the remainder of his journey broke down he was compelled to join the Marquis. Before reporting to a British officer at Decize on 30 September 1944, he took part in four battles against the Germans in the area south-west of Toulouse. This solo escape into Switzerland by a private soldier was a first class performance.

As well as campaign medals, many of the territorials who had enlisted in the TA just prior to the Second World War became eligible for the award of the Territorial Efficiency Medal. This award was normally given for twelve years' service but, as war service counted as double, they qualified after six years. This precedent had been established after the First World War. Apart from 43rd RTR still serving in India, the 'Weekend Warriors' from the Tyne to Tweed stood down again in 1945 and went home. As Jimmy Charter said, 'It was the longest annual camp I had ever been to!'

NINE

THE TERRITORIAL ARMY
1947–1967

When the red light comes on we are ready;
For the sergeant to shout 'Number One';
Though we sit in a plane altogether,
We all tumble out one by one.

Anon.

The Territorial Army was officially reconstituted on 1 January 1947. It had been in abeyance since 2 September 1939, which provided for a National Army, and suspended the TA as an independent distinctive entity. The original concept in 1947 was to build up a field force capable of instant readiness for overseas service. The force, consisting of two armoured Divisions and nine infantry Divisions, was to be commanded by officers and NCOs with war service. These would be found from volunteers and National Service men, National Service having been introduced in 1948 when the wartime call-up system ceased, and the force would be fully trained after full-time service in regular units. They would be available from 1950.

It was a period dominated by relations with the Soviet Union. From reforming in 1947 to the mid-1950s, another European war seemed likely. The Berlin Airlift of 1948 and the Korean War of 1950–1953 were periods when tension was at a peak. That tension gradually reduced as the 1950s progressed. In 1956 the NS commitment that men must take part in two weeks' training in an annual camp was ended and, with the abolition of National Service in 1960, the Territorial Army became solely volunteer. It was also the beginning of constant change. From then on the emphasis shifted to Home Defence – the original role of the Territorial Force of 1908. Only two TA divisions – 43rd (Wessex) and 53rd (Welsh) – were to be retained at full scale to complete the British contingent required to carry out our NATO commitments.

Once again the dilapidated, unfurnished Drill Halls were being opened up, and some of the wartime damage was being repaired, although a shortage of building materials caused some problems. Regular commanding officers, quartermasters, training majors and senior NCOs, in a Permanent Staff Instructor (PSI) role, began returning to the pre-war locations of the TA in Newcastle and Northumberland. Wartime rationing was maintained well into the 1950s. There is the true story of a lady who walked into a local Drill Hall just at the moment that a brigadier, with his retinue, who was carrying out his first annual inspection, was walking down the stairs in the hall. She asked the highly embarrassed PSI, 'Is this the place where you can buy the blankets?' The brigadier was rather taken aback but it is not recorded what he said later. At his first annual camp at Barnard Castle, County Durham, in 1951, a young recruit can recall handing his sweet coupons to the NAAFI girl behind the counter for some chocolate and being told that he did not need coupons there. He took a suitcase half-full of chocolate home with him at the end of the camp.

'Moving with the times'. The old Artillery Drill Hall on Barrack Road, Newcastle. It is now named 'Barrack Court'. (W. Morton)

Sergeant R. Middleton (left) and Colour Sergeant R. Jackson, both of 17 Para Battalion, c.1952. (R. Jackson)

Many pre-war territorials returned to their old Drill Halls and signed on again. Some of them had fought hard and bitter wars, and some of them had been Prisoners of War of the Germans and Japanese. Among them were John Donald, Chris Mitchelson and Joe Purvis DCM, who had all been taken at St Valery, France, in 1940. Others were Norman Cosgrove and Norman 'Dinkie' Middleton, who had spent over three years as prisoners of the Japanese and suffered accordingly. There were also those from other counties of the British Isles who had served in the North East, met and married local girls, then settled down in the home town or village of their wife.

There were numerous anti-aircraft regiments reformed but the Air Defence System was soon to be dismantled and they were either amalgamated or disbanded. The following list gives the Order of Battle of the auxiliary forces in Newcastle and Northumberland, c.1947:

ALNWICK: One troop, 'C' Squadron, Northumberland Hussars. Headquarters, 7/RNF.

AMBLE: 'C' Company, 7/RNF.

ASHINGTON: 'C' Squadron, NH, 'B' Company, 7/RNF.

BERWICK: 'R' Battery, 670 Light Anti-Aircraft Battery RA, 'D' Company, 7/RNF.

BLYTH: 'P' Battery, 272 Field Regiment, RA, 405 Heavy Ack-Ack Regt.

GOSFORTH: 324 Heavy Ack-Ack Regt; 36 (M) Signal Squadron Royal Signals; 149 Field Ambulance, RAMC; 102 Field Security Section, RMP; 36 (M) Signals Squadron. Royal Signals (ATS).

HALTWHISTLE: 'Y' Company, 4/RNF.

HEATON: 'R' Battery, 537 Searchlight Regt RA; HQ, 104 Army Regt RE; 86 (AGRA) Field Workshops, REME; 109 Field Security Section, RMP.

HEXHAM: HQ, 4/RNF.

MORPETH: 'A' Company, 7/RNF.

NEWBURN: 'S' Company and 'X' Company, 4/RNF.

NEWCASTLE: HQ, NH; 43rd Royal Tank Regiment; 272 Field Regt RA; HQ HQ, 670 Light Ack-Ack Regt RA; 103 Engineer Regt RE 'A' Company, 17th Battalion, Parachute Regiment 552 (GT) Company, RASC; 1 (N) General Hospital RAMC; Durham University Officers Training Corps; 3508 Fighter Control Unit, (RAAF) RAF; RAF Reserve Centre, RAAF.

NORTH SHIELDS: HQ, 404 Coast Regt RA

OUSTON: 607 Squadron, RAAF.

PRUDHOE: 'Z' Company, 4/RNF.

SEATON DELAVAL: 405 Heavy Ack-Ack Regt RA.

TYNEMOUTH: HQ, 537 Searchlight Regt RA; Engineer Squadron, 104 Army Engineer Regt RE; 128 E&M Squadron, REME.

WALKER: 588 Light Ack-Ack Regt RA

WALLSEND: 508 Field Squadron, 103 Field Engineer Regt RE.

WESTERHOPE: 'Q' Battery, 670 Light Ack-Ack Regt RA; 505 Field
                   Squadron, 103 Field Engineer Regt RE.

WHITLEY BAY: HQ, 464 Heavy Ack-Ack Regt RA.

A new Auxiliary Territorial Service (ATS), which had been raised in the build-up of the TA just prior the war, was playing an active role in the post-war renaissance. The first ATS unit from Tyne to Tweed was 40 Company, ATS, under the command of a Mrs Ramsden, which started its drill nights and training in Fenham Barracks in 1939. Sandhurst Block – the only part of the barracks now remaining – became a training centre for the ATS later in the war. Women played a vital part in the manning of Air Defence Great Britain, with Royal Artillery units, as they did in many other units at home and abroad. Quite a few served in the 53rd Searchlight Regiment.

The first annual camps in 1947 were voluntary. In some cases the units had barely enough members to carry out the normal routine of camp duties, and the training was very basic. According to *St George's Gazette*, September 1947, 151 Infantry Brigade was the only TA formation to go into camp that year, at RAF Boulmer, Northumberland. Northumberland and Durham territorials were giving a lead to the rest of the country. In camp were 4/RNF, 7/RNF, 6/DLI, 8/DLI, and 17/Parachute Battalion, formerly 9/DLI. 7/RNF could only muster six officers and sixty-five men. So it can be seen that 1947 was a year of rebuilding and regeneration. The social side had been restarted and efforts were being made to restore the pre-war sense of pride and comradeship in the various units. Regimental colours were restored to the infantry battalions from where they had been lodged at the start of the war in 1939. Hexham Abbey had held the colours of 4/RNF; 7/RNF retrieved their colours from St James' church, in Morpeth, and their Northumbrian Pipes from Hedgeley Hall. In Newcastle 43rd Tanks recovered their colours from St Thomas church, and 588 Light Anti-Aircraft Regiment (formerly 5/RNF) reclaimed theirs from Walker parish church. These same colours were later laid up in their respective parish churches.

As a royal recognition of the contribution of the Territorial Army in 1939–1945, King George VI reviewed representative detachments of every element of the TA in Hyde Park, London, on Sunday 31 October 1948. Following the issue of the blue beret to replace the old khaki beret in 1950, a Regimental Order was issued to all RNF Battalions, 'as a consequence of the regiment being issued with a blue beret and red and white hackle the gosling green patch with the red 'V' will cease to be worn'. This patch had been worn on the upper part of both sleeves of the battle dress blouse, and behind the cap badge on the khaki beret. The red Roman numeral V designated the regiment's precedence as the Fifth of Foot. Now it would be distinguished by the red-over-white hackle. Replacing the khaki service dress (SD) introduced in 1902, the ubiquitous khaki battle dress was first issued in May 1939. This drab serge uniform was meant to have drab badges and other insignia with thin, coloured arm of service stripes, such as scarlet for the infantry, red and yellow for the RAC, blue and white for RS, blue and red for RA, and red, blue and yellow from the REME, worn at the top of both sleeves. Over the years, formation signs, such as divisional and other patches, were added. Other items such as coloured lanyards, and the fact that cavalry regiments had defied Dress Regulations and wore metal insignia, changed the whole concept of battle dress. After National Service ended, the khaki No.2 Dress was issued to the Regular Army. The TA wore battle dress until the changes in 1968, when it began to be issued to members of the newly formed Territorial & Volunteer Army Reserve (T & AVR).

After reforming in 1947, 4/RNF and 7/RNF were part of 151 (North Durham) Brigade, together with 8/DLI. The first reductions among the artillery started in 1950 when 588 Light Anti-Aircraft Regiment RA (RNF), based at Walker, amalgamated with 4/RNF to form 4/5RNF. It was not until 1956, with the conversion of 43rd Tanks in Newcastle back to their original infantry role as 6/RNF, that the three battalions came together in their old formation as 149 Brigade, thus regaining their pre-1938, 50th Division affiliation. They were joined in 1960 by 4/Border Regiment, making it a four-battalion brigade as it had been in 1914. Over a period of two years, 1954 to 1956, a number of reorganisations took place among the artillery units. At Tynemouth, 537 Searchlight Regiment, which had been formed from the Tyne Electrics, was amalgamated with 669 (Durham) and 670 (Tyneside Scottish) LAA/Regiments to form 439 LAA/Regiment RA (TA), with headquarters at Tynemouth, with 'P' and 'Q' (Tyne Electrical Engineers) Batteries, 'R' (South Shields) Battery, and 'S' (Tyneside Scottish) Battery, in 1955. This was swiftly followed in 1956 by amalgamating with 404 Coast Regiment RA (TA), and being renamed as 439 (Tyne) LAA/Regiment (TA), with 404 Regiment becoming 'Q' (Tynemouth) Battery. These artillery regiments must have been in a constant state of flux, and the personnel extremely annoyed.

In 1947, 405 Coast Regiment had been raised at Blyth, and then moved to Gosforth. It was renamed as 405 Heavy Anti-Aircraft Regiment RA (Tynemouth) (TA) in 1948. Then, in 1954, this unit merged with 464 (M) Heavy Anti-Aircraft Regiment RA (Northumbrian) Field Regiment (TA), with no change of title. The old 72 (Northumbrian) Field Regiment RA (TA) in Barrack Road Drill Hall, was

From top to bottom: Sergeant 'Old' Geordie Jackson, L/Cpl Sammy Jackson (brother), Sergeant Ralph Jackson (brother), Fusilier 'Young' Geordie Jackson (son of 'Old' Geordie), c.1948. (R. Jackson)

reconstituted as 272 Field Regiment RA (TA) in 1947. The 1939 duplicate of the 72nd was re-raised in 1947 as 324 Heavy Air Defence Regiment RA (Northumbrian) (TA), with headquarters at Gosforth. It was merged with 405 (HAA) in 1955 with no change of title. 670 (LAA) Regiment RA (TA), which had been formed by the reconstitution and conversion of the 1st Battalion, Tyneside Scottish, the Black Watch (Royal Highland Regiment) based in Newcastle, had a distinguished lineage, with its origins in the volunteer movement of 1859 as a kilted company of the Newcastle Rifle Volunteers. This company eventually lost its distinctive Highland dress and Scottish links. Raised again in 1914 as the 20th to 23rd Battalions, The Northumberland Fusiliers, (1st to 4th Battalions, Tyneside Scottish), it was disbanded in 1918. In 1939 it was raised as a battalion of the Durham Light Infantry, but became affiliated to the Black Watch and adopted the Black Watch tartan regimental arm patch, and traditional tam o'shanter with the red hackle.

Another unit which had been reformed on 13 August 1947 was the 1st Northern General Hospital RAMC (TA), under the command of Colonel A. Angus. It was situated in the Militia Camp which had been built in 1939. This hutted camp was situated across the road from Fenham Barracks, next to the Garrison Sports Ground. It was bounded by Ponteland Road, Brighton Grove, Nun's Moor Park, and Studely Terrace. Recruiting was very slow in the initial stages and it was very close to being disbanded, but a concerted effort was made to keep the unit going, and numbers gradually improved. Eventually it moved into the barracks and occupied the Hospital Block. Also based in the Militia Camp was 552 (GT) Company, RASC (TA), and 'A' Company, 17 Parachute Battalion, The Parachute Regiment (TA), which later moved its headquarters to Gateshead. The camp was handed back to Newcastle City Council in 1956, and was subsequently demolished.

Sergeant Norman 'Dinky' Middleton, a small, slight man, transferred from the Fusiliers together with his brother, Sergeant Ray Middleton, and Colour Sergeant Ralph Jackson to 17/Para. He told a story of a training jump from a captive balloon. He was first to jump out of the basket and the instructor told him to shout to release the tension. He said, 'I screamed my bloody head off, I was terrified.' Owing to his light weight the others were passing him in mid-air. An officer on the ground giving advice through a loud-hailer asked him, 'Are you going to stay up there all day?'

Owing to the international situation with respect to the tension with the Soviet Union and the Korean War, it was decided by the government in 1951 that Class 'Z' Reservists should be recalled for two weeks refresher training with the Territorial Army units at annual camps, in order to bring them up to war strength. Thousands of reservists were involved. In some cases as many as 700 reservists were needed to bring units up to their war establishment. Some of them were very unhappy, as were their wives or girlfriends. Many of them had been PoWs and thought they had been punished enough. However, in the

A smart group of RAMC (TA), 1st Northern General Hospital. They are probably ex-NS men. (W. Morton)

main the scheme went off with reasonable success. It placed a heavy burden on the normal administration of the TA. The reservist had to be documented, clothed and equipped, fed and housed, and war scales of weapons, ammunition, and vehicles had to be drawn from Ordnance Depots. It was good training, and an education for the territorials as well. This exercise was repeated again in 1952 but with far fewer numbers. As with all large-scale army exercises, there were casualties of some sort. In one case it was a reservist with 4/5 RNF. The *Newcastle Journal*, 29 September 1952, noted that: 'Fusilier Daniel Damson an ex-PoW aged 33, from Haltwhistle, died on a training exercise on Bellerby Ranges.' An obituary in the *St George's Gazette*, October 1952, states,

> We are sorry to record that 4274936 Fusilier Daniel Dawson of Greencroft, Haltwhistle, died at annual camp. Fusilier Dawson was ex-9th Battalion, and had been a Prisoner of War in Japanese hands. He leaves a wife and young daughter. To his wife and family we tender our deepest sympathy. The sum of £30 was contributed by all ranks of HQ, 151 Brigade (TA) and the battalion for the family of Fusilier Dawson.'

On 1 May 1947 the old Tyne Electrical Engineers reformed as the following units: 104 Army Engineers Regiment RE (TA), 128 Electrical and Mechanical Squadron RE, Tyne Electrical Engineers (TA) and 86 (Field) AGRA Workshop REME (TA), with headquarters at Debdon Gardens, Heaton and Tynemouth. An early casualty of the recruit shortage was 104 (AE) Regiment. In October 1947 the unit had nine officers and seventeen sappers; on 28 November 1948 the strength was still nine officers, but one man had been lost, and it had recruited only 2 per cent of its establishment. So, in July 1950, 104 Regiment was absorbed by 105 Corps Engineer Regiment RE (TA). The other Engineer Regiment in the area was 50th (Northumbrian) Divisional Engineers (TA), with its headquarters at Barras Bridge in Newcastle. This Engineer unit was descended from the old Newcastle Engineer Volunteer Company formed at the Elswick Works of Armstrong, Whitworth & Mitchell in 1860, which had been based in Barras Bridge Drill Hall since its move from the Elswick Works in 1862. In May 1947 the unit was re-established at Barras Bridge. As Divisional Engineers were then being designated as regiments, the new title was 103 Field Engineer Regiment RE (TA). Its sub-units were 235 Field Park Squadron at Westerhope, and 506 Field Squadron at Wallsend, where they occupied the former Northumberland Fusiliers Drill Hall.

For the territorials of Northumberland and Tyneside, the 1950s and 1960s were periods of great ceremonial occasions, and great change. The Coronation of Her Majesty Queen Elizabeth II took place in 1953, as did the Divisional exercise on Salisbury Plain. Her visit to Newcastle in 1954 was greeted by a guard of honour mounted by 4/5 RNF (TA) with the massed bands – ninety strong and in full dress – of 1/RNF and 4/5 RNF (TA), with a royal salute fired by 272 (Northumbrian) Field Regiment RA (TA). Annual camps for 1955 were cancelled due to a strike by railway workers. The Freedom of Morpeth was granted to 7/RNF in 1957. The Golden Jubilee of the Territorial Army was celebrated in 1958, with a review by Queen Elizabeth II in Hyde Park; and in June of that year she visited Holy Island, where a guard of honour was mounted by 7/RNF (TA), with the band of 6/RNF (TA). But perhaps one of the most significant events as far as the RNF were concerned was a spectacular presentation of new colours by Field Marshal Sir Francis Festing GCB, KBE, DSO, to 7/RNF on Friday 8 September 1961. The presentation took place in the Outer-Bailey of Alnwick Castle by permission of His Grace the 10th Duke of Northumberland KG, TD, JP, the Honorary Colonel of 7/RNF. Officers carrying the new colours were 2nd/Lieutenant R. Scott, Queen's colour, 2nd/Lieutenant T.D. Stirk, Regimental colour. The old colours were borne by Lieutenant F. Calvert, King's colour, and 2nd/Lieutenant R.G. Turnbull, Regimental colour. These old colours had been presented at Windsor Castle by King Edward VII in 1909. Following a march through Berwick-upon-Tweed on Saturday 9 September, to exercise the regiment's right to march through the town with colours flying, drums beating and

Above left: *Sergeant N. 'Dinky' Middleton, ex-PoW of Japanese, served on Burma Railway ex-9th RNF Camp, c.1948. (R. Middleton)*

Above right: *National Serviceman Bill Morton, who had served in Korea in 1951, and was at Aldershot on his TA service after demob, c.1953. (W. Morton)*

Warrant Officers and Sergeants of 7th RNF (TA), annual camp at Barnard Castle, 1951. 'Z' Reservists are not wearing scarlet sashes. (R. Jackson)

bayonets fixed, on Sunday 10 September the old colours were laid up in St Michael's church, Alnwick. This was the last pair of colours presented to any battalion of the regiment before amalgamation. The 1961 colours can be seen laid up in the entrance hall of Alnwick Castle. 2nd/Lieutenants R. Scott and R.G. Turnbull were to achieve the rank of Lieutenant Colonel; R. Scott as commanding officer of 6/RRF, and Turnbull commanding Northumbrian University Officers Training Corps.

At that time 7/RNF was commanded by Lieutenant Colonel J.I.M. Smail MC, TD. A New Zealander, he was a trifle unorthodox, but a tremendous leader. He was bluntly spoken, but was a man of legendary generosity, and a staunch friend. When he was relinquishing his command in 1963, he spoke to Sergeant Wilfie Sword, who was a pre-war territorial, and said, 'I am sorry that you are leaving the battalion Sergeant Sword'. Wilfie replied, 'But aam not gannin sor'. 'Jim', as the Lieutenant Colonel was known to all ranks, replied, 'You bloody well are you know! I'm taking all you old buggers with me'. A lot went with Wilfie. During Exercise *Overlord II*, described in chapter 3, one of the fusiliers decided that he liked a barometer in the shape of a bottle opener advertising Guinness, hanging in a pub. After the constable closed the bar at about 3 a.m. because somebody had pinched his hat – and the pub had run out of beer anyway – the landlord reported the barometer missing. On battalion muster parade on the Sunday morning, 'Jim' addressed the battalion, saying, 'Alright, who's got the bloody barometer? You'd better get the bugger back or you're all for it'. It miraculously appeared in one of the company lines. The reason why the pubs were still open was because the tide was in and the island was cut of from the mainland.

4th/5th Battalion., Hexham, c.1953. From right to left: CSM 'Chuck' Chambers, CSM Mike Delaney, CSM 'Barney' King, Sergeant Jack Walker and Sergeant Norman Roberts. (T. Hewitson)

Panoramic view of presentation of new colours to 7th RNF by Field Marshal Sir Francis Festing, 8 September 1961, Alnwick Castle: 'Colour being blessed'. (J.I.M. Small)

There was great rivalry among the three Fusilier Battalions. The city boys from the 'Toon' (Newcastle) tended to look askance at the pit yackers and farm boys of the mining and rural companies, although it must be said that 4/5 RNF, 7/RNF and 4/Border got on well together, being from the same social background. It is often said that a 'Geordie' is just a Northumbrian with his brains kicked out! During annual camp at Thetford, Norfolk, in 1962, the author, as guard commander of 7/RNF, was heavily involved in pacifying a mob of irate young fusiliers from 6/RNF who were intent on having a crack at some of 7/RNF whom they accused of beating up one of their company. It was a tense and fraught few minutes before order was restored.

Civil defence training became part of the training cycle of all TA units. One annual camp in four was to be devoted to civil defence, and odd weekends were spent at the Civil Defence Training Centre at Ponteland, and later at Morpeth. Although the training was demanding, and would have been of great importance in the case of air assault and nuclear attack – if anyone had survived – it was seen by many of those serving as being an inappropriate role for a territorial. Uniformed civil defence units had not been disbanded at this stage, and in some instances they shared garage space with their local TA unit. One TA garage, which will be not be identified, contained TA half-tracks, Land Rovers and 3-ton trucks. It also housed a very large civil defence rescue vehicle fitted out with rescue equipment, ladders and so on. Unfortunately, when they came to drive it out for an exercise one weekend, it would not start. It did not take them long to discover that one of the TA drivers, while doing routine maintenance, had been topping up his petrol tank from the civil defence vehicle tanks. The same driver painted his Hillman car with army-green paint used on the vehicles. Unfortunately, the car was the same model as was being used as an army staff car at that period. Another brigadier on his annual inspection demanded that the PSI tell him how he had managed to acquire a buckshee staff car.

In the mid-fifties and early sixties, it was quite evident that the politicians were hellbent on getting rid of what they probably regarded as an anachronism. Socialist politicians have never cared much for the armed services. Anything of a militaristic nature is anathema. The introduction of the Territorial Army Emergency Reserve ('Ever Readies') in 1962 was the start of the demise of the TA as it was then constituted. Many will argue that it was badly equipped – which was true – under-trained and under-manned. What they forgot was that a large number of ex-National Servicemen were still serving in the TA. Many of them had seen active service in Malaya, Korea, Kenya, the Canal Zone, Egypt, Suez and Cyprus. Virtually every element of the TA had men who undertook the TAER obligation, although it has to be said there were some who only joined for the £150 bounty. The last thing they wanted was to be called up for six months' service, or take part in the training opportunities abroad that were offered in addition to their annual camp.

Pipers John and Fred Redpath, and John Mackintosh, of 7th RNF at Brecon Camp, 1963. They are wearing 'Shepherd's Plaid' as worn by the Duke of Northumberland's personal piper. (F. Redpath)

However, many 'Ever Readies' took the opportunity to spend two-week attachments with regular units. The majority were with the British Army of the Rhine (BAOR) but a number served in Aden during the turbulent period just prior to granting independence and withdrawing British forces in 1967. Some, from the south of England, were mobilised for six months, but the majority were there for two-week periods attached to regular units. The calling up of territorials for Afghanistan in 2002 was claimed to be the first time since 1945 – not so! What happened to the TA after the implementation of the 'Reserve Forces Act' of 1966 has already been explained in chapter 3. Not only the TA was affected: The Civil Defence Corps, and the Auxiliary Fire Service were also disbanded; and the Royal Observer Corps suffered severe cut backs. Apart from the TAVR III element, the only remaining infantry company in Northumberland and Newcastle was 'A' Company, of the Fusilier Volunteers, which was formed from the three old RNF Battalions and based in St George's Drill Hall, Newcastle, which was later demolished, and is now a University car park.

This company was amalgamated with fusilier companies from Warwickshire (two companies), London (one) and Lancashire (one), to form a TAVR II Battalion from 1 April 1967. 'A' Company was commanded by Major Frank Potts of Stanton, near Longhorsely. His is one of the many cases of family continuity within the old TA of fathers and sons, brothers and cousins, serving together. He had commanded the same fusilier company as his father before him. His brother Roger also served, and the same company was later commanded by his nephew, Chester Potts, with Patrick Scott as his second in command, the son of Colonel Robert Scott who commanded the same company after Major Potts. The cap badge of the Fusilier Brigade was worn by the Fusilier Volunteers, but each company retained its old hackle: in 'A' Company the red and white of the RNF was worn; 'HQ' and 'B' Companies wore the blue and gold of the Warwicks; 'C' Company wore the primrose hackle of the Lancashire Fusiliers and 'D' Company, the white of the Royal Fusiliers. This was changed in 1968 when all the companies adopted the red and white of the RNF, the senior regiment.

The gunners were the only ones to arrive at a satisfactory conclusion with the amalgamation of 272 Field Regiment, 274 Field Regiment, 324 Heavy Air Defence Regiment and 439 (Tyne) Light Air Defence Regiment to form 101 (Northumbrian) Medium Field Regiment RA (V), contained in the old Drill Hall on Barrack Road. The local artillery regiments had always been extremely well-trained and very efficient. They needed to be – they could do an extraordinary amount of damage to their own troops if shells dropped short of the target. It was not only the infantry and the gunners who had to face up to the challenge of the wholesale reorganisation of the territorial regiments from Tyne to Tweed. Engineer units were to be reduced and amalgamated so that on 1 April 1967, 72 Engineer Regiment (T&AVR)

Colour Sergeant,
T. Hewitson, 7th
RNF, 'Ever Ready'.
Attached to 9 Platoon,
'Y' Company.
1st RNF, Aden,
November 1966.
On stop-and-search
operation in Crater.
(J. Hall)

could rise from the ashes. On 1 April the regiment was composed of: RHQ, 72 Engineer Regiment (Tyne Electrical Engineers) (V) Gateshead, 103 (1st Newcastle) Field Squadron RE (V) Newcastle, 105 (Durham) Plant Squadron RE (V) South Shields, 118 (Tees) Field Squadron RE (V) Hartlepool, 129 (East Riding) Field Squadron RE (V) Hull and 72 Engineer Regiment Workshop REME (V) Gateshead. As can be seen, this geographical spread could cause some problems with control and command and meant a lot of travel for the permanent staff. These problems were also to be found in the newly formed Fusilier Volunteer Battalion, with companies spread from Newcastle to London. The resulting claims for travel allowances and overnight claims by the permanent staff, and others, must have made a mockery of calls for economic stringency. So the new, slimmed-down, leaner and fitter Territorial & Army Volunteer Reserve came into being.

TEN

THE NEW TERRITORIALS
1967–2004

The politicians said you're not needed now so we went away,
But you can bet they'll turn around to call us back some day;
Will we go? I don't know? They didn't want us then,
Instead of us we'll send them, we won't need soldiers then.

T. L. Hewitson, 2004.

So far, the scope of this account has been focused on the area from Tyne to Tweed. But with the radical restructuring of the Territorial Army in 1967–68, that title seems inappropriate, such has been the change during the years that have elapsed since then. Not only have the units gone through some dramatic cutbacks in their recent history, but the old County Territorial Associations have changed out of all recognition. Northumberland County Territorial Association, after periods of restructuring and mergers, is now known as The Reserve Forces and Cadets Association for the North of England, based in Durham City, encompassing Northumberland, Tyne & Wear, County Durham and Teeside.

In many ways, the changes have been beneficial to some units. One of them was the 1st Northern General Hospital, RAMC (V) (TAVR), based in Fenham Barracks. From 1 April 1967 the unit was retitled as 201 (Northern) General Hospital, RAMC (V) (TAVR) and was amalgamated with 149 Field Ambulance RAMC (TA). A move was made from the old Hospital Block, later demolished, into Sandhurst Block within the barracks. A detachment was established in January 1979 in the new TA Centre – as the old Drill Halls had been renamed – built at Cramlington, and another was formed at Coulby

Newham on Teeside in 1982. The Gulf War in 1991 created an awareness of the lack of specialists that had been caused by the over-enthusiastic government cutbacks, and the Ministry of Defence had to make recourse to the territorials for replacements. Accordingly, volunteers were called for from RAMC units. Some 80 per cent of members of 201 volunteered for active service. In the event, eighteen male and fourteen female members served in the Gulf. One hundred and ninety-five years after the 1st Newcastle Engineer Volunteers had volunteered to serve in the Egyptian campaign of 1886, the 'Medics' from Newcastle went to war in the Middle East.

The 201 Hospital had been granted the Freedom of Newcastle-upon-Tyne on 25 July 1984, which was accepted by HRH Queen Elizabeth, the Queen Mother. She said at the ceremony:

> It is of special significance that this distinction should come not only on the 150th anniversary of the medical school [in Newcastle] but also on the 75 years since the formation of the General Service Hospital Corps. Since these beginnings you have served your country with courage and distinction at home and overseas in two world wars and in times of peace.

The 'Medics' of today also play a part in supporting events within the civil community as well as using their medical expertise for military purposes. The British intervention in the Balkans has seen volunteers from 201 out in the field providing medical services for the regular forces and the locals alike. With the capability to set up an 800-bed hospital – although the *Sunday Express*, 24 March 2002, claimed that this was to be reduced to a 400-bed capacity – and with detachments now at Newton Aycliffe and Stockton-on-Tees, this unit is one of the success stories of the modern Territorial Army. As a refreshing spin-off from their normal duties, some of the female members took up training, guided by Staff Sergeant M. Thornton, a PSI, and formed a tug-of-war team representing 201. There were no male volunteers! The team was very successful and won a number of events in various competitions. In 1997 they won a gold prize at 39 Regiment, Royal Artillery reunion open day, and were also 480kg champions at the Army Medical Services championships, against regular competition. They were 520 and 560kg champions and, at the Aldershot Horse Show Open Tug of War Competition, they were 560kg champions for 1998 and 1999. Silver prizes for the same events were won in 2000. As Staff Sergeant Thornton remarked, 'All squads were larger than 201 with more and better training facilities, we had a tree, a 500 metre bungee and the Town Moor'.

The reorganisation of the Engineers brought 29 Engineer Brigade from Edinburgh to Fenham Barracks, where they set up shop in the old Clock Block in

The ladies' Tug of War team of 201 Field Hospital RAMC (V). Staff Sergeant M. Thornton, Trainer, is in the centre of the back row. (M. Thornton)

Rededicating the guns: Tynemouth Castle, 4 May 1985. 101 (Northumbrian) Regiment RA (V). (J. Winter)

Fenham Barracks – also demolished later – as parent unit to 72 Engineer Regiment. With the bulk of the new TAVR II units being earmarked for the reinforcement of BAOR, Geoffrey Rippon, the Conservative shadow Defence Minister, in a debate on 4 March 1969, remarked, 'We alone of all countries in Western Europe have virtually no home defence of any kind.' By 1972 the regiment had 124 Corps Recovery Company (Tyne Electrical Engineers) REME (V) at Newton Aycliffe added to its establishment. The engineers achieved another first in 1977: 193 Field Squadron became part of the Harrier Jet Support Group working with the RAF and Regular Engineers, constructing and maintaining landing sites. The regiment was also closely involved with local authorities and voluntary organisations giving assistance with all sorts of building and engineering projects. 129 Field Squadron was transferred to 73 Engineer Regiment RE (V). Once again, the Engineers were involved in constructing stands for a colour presentation. In 1961, TA Engineers had constructed stands for 7/RNF at Alnwick Castle. In 1978, their successors, 6/RRF, who were to receive new colours, called upon the services of the TAVR Engineers, commanded by Lieutenant Colonel L. McLeman, to carry out the same task. On the non-engineering side, the Regimental Pipe Band was always in demand. The pipers were a regular part of the annual celebrations in Hamelin, Germany.

The same mid-week cycle of training in TA Centres with weekends spent out in the field enhancing their skills, followed by two weeks' annual camp where they put into practice what they had learned over the training year, is basically no different to the routine carried out by the Territorial Army of the past. The difference now is that they have a superior equipment scale and enough transport is held to carry out realistic training, although with new methods of keeping transport in a pool from which units can draw vehicles this will change. In fact, this is precisely the same method that was used in the 1950s! Transport problems sometimes arise due to constraints on fuel allocations; nothing really changes. There is also the fact that TA members who are drivers in the civilian occupation are bound by health and safety legislation, which means that if a driver has completed a specified number of hours driving in his day job, he cannot drive for the TA on his days off. So the army vehicles remain stationary. Another aspect of health and safety today is risk assessment. Everything they do is subject to this procedure. If European legislation and health and safety regulations are carried out to the letter, then it seems probable that the conduct of military operations in the future will be seriously hampered. Will it be impossible to fight? Service personnel should realise the risk inherent in handling lethal weapons and explosives – they should not need to be told.

The gunners were more or less sorted out although vastly reduced numerically. 101 (Northumbrian) Field Regiment, Royal Artillery (V), was given recognition

Pipes and drums, 72 Engineer Regiment (V), Hamelin, Germany, 1980. Pipe Major Fred Redpath is on the right flank, and his brother John is on the left. (F. Redpath)

of 120 years connection and service to the City of Newcastle, in October 1980, when the City Council granted them the Freedom of the City and the, 'privilege, honour and distinction of marching through the streets of the City on all ceremonial occasions with bayonets fixed, colours flying and bands playing'. At that time the regiment was composed of RHQ and HQ Battery at Barrack Road, Newcastle, 203 (Elswick) Field Battery, Cowpen Road, Blyth, 204 (Tyneside Scottish) Field Battery, Walker, 205 (3rd Durham Volunteer Artillery) Field Battery, Northfield Gardens, South Shields, and Light Aid Detachment, REME, Gosforth. 101 Field Regiment was recruited to 96 per cent of its establishment, equipped with 105mm Light Guns and designated for service in BAOR in the event of war. In the 1967 reductions the Tyneside Scottish Battery, then 'Q' Battery, of 439 LAA Regiment was, for a short period, absorbed as 'D' Company in the 4th/5th/6th (Territorial) Battalion, RNF (TAVR III), before being reunited with the Royal Artillery. Today, the regiment is the only territorial artillery regiment to be equipped with the Multi-Launch Rocket

System (MLRS) in the British Army. The regiment's sub-units are now based in: 101 Regimental Headquarters and Headquarters Battery, Gateshead; 203 (Elswick) Battery, Blyth; 204 (Tyneside Scottish) Battery; REME Workshop and RLC Stores Section at Kingston Park, Newcastle; 205 (3rd Durham) Battery, South Shields.

RSM Thornton, first RSM of 6th Battalion Royal Regiment of Fusiliers. (D.M. Thornton)

Princess Royal at a Save the Children fête, at Alnwick Castle, Wednesday 13 July 1990. Drummers of 6 RRF (V) are sounding a fanfare.

Of all the former TA regiments between the Tyne and Tweed, it was the infantry that bore the brunt of the cuts initially. The three former RNF battalions were reduced to one TAVR II Company in Newcastle, and the 4th/5th/6th and 7th (Territorial) Battalions, RNF; both TAVR III Battalions with an eight-day annual camp and no entitlement to bounties. These two TAVR III units were reduced to eight-man cadres in 1968, and one company was kept going at Ashington, Northumberland, and had been kept going on a voluntary basis, largely unpaid, by a hardcore group of enthusiastic senior NCOs led by Major (later Lieutenant-Colonel) Robert Scott. As a result of their determination, and the realisation that one of the major recruiting areas in the UK had been decimated, a major rethink was called for on the part of the Royal Regiment Fusiliers and the Ministry of Defence. It was not only the fault of the MOD, but also the upper echelons of the newly formed Royal Regiment of Fusiliers. At this time there was a lot of ill feeling, and acrimonious exchanges were taking place between the old regiments and the new, so some concessions were made. The Fusilier Volunteer Battalion became the 5th Battalion, RRF (Volunteers). On 1 April 1968, the Fusiliers at Ashington had their dedication recognised by becoming 'E' Company, 5/RRF, in 1969. As with the other widespread units in the North East, there were logistical and administrative problems caused by the huge geographical area covered by this battalion.

The eight-man cadres of the former TAVR III Battalions in the North East were formed into a multi-badged unit designated as The Northumbrian Volunteers, TAVR II, on 1 April 1971, with the 4th/5th/6th RNF Cadre being 'C' Company, and the 7th RNF Cadre becoming 'D' Company. Headquarters of this battalion was at Bishop Auckland, County Durham, and its first commanding officer was Lieutenant Colonel C.A.F. Baker-Cresswell, living in Bamburgh, Northumberland. A former Rifle Brigade officer, he had been serving as a Major with 7/RNF when everything fell to pieces. A more committed officer could not have been found; he was an iron fist in a velvet glove. He was to play a prominent part in Regimental and County Territorial Army affairs in later years.

Recognition of the administrative and logistical difficulties of maintaining an efficient level of control over an area stretching from Balham in London to Ashington in Northumberland, was perhaps the reason for the formation of a new Fusilier Battalion in the Tyne–Tweed area on 1 April 1975. This was the 6th Battalion, The Royal Regiment of Fusiliers (Volunteers). It was formed from 'A' and 'E' Companies of 5/RRF and 'C' and 'D' Companies of The Northumbrian Volunteers. Another controversial figure came back to Alnwick as the 6th Battalion's first Regimental Sergeant Major. He was W.O.1. D.M. Thornton. As a young man serving an apprenticeship as a shipwright at Walker Naval Yard, he had enlisted in the 43rd Tanks (TA) in Newcastle. When the 43rd reverted to its former infantry role in 1956, he transferred to 'A' Company, 17 Para, at the Militia Camp. Called up for National Service in 1958 at the age of twenty-one, he later opted to stay in the army. His first tour with the TA was as PSI with 'B' Company, 7/RNF from 1965 to 1967. An outspoken person, not always popular with some of the officers, he was highly regarded by the members of the company. His eventual appointment as RSM was not without some opposition from some of the old guard, but wiser heads prevailed. He left the battalion in 1976, and returned as Quartermaster in 1983. He retired from the Army as a Major in 1986, but continued working with a TA unit as PSAO until reaching Army retirement age.

The companies of 6/RRF were redesignated as 'X' and 'Y', both based in Newcastle, 'Z' at Ashington, with HQ at Alnwick and Berwick. In 1978 'W' was established at Berwick and Alnwick. The first major ceremony in which the 6th Battalion was involved was the presentation of new colours by HRH The Duke of Kent GCMG, GCVO, ADC, on 6 October 1978 at Alnwick Castle. In 1979 the designation TAVR was replaced by the old title of TA. Exercise *Crusader* in 1980 was the battalion's first major deployment in Germany. This was due to its role as reinforcement for BAOR, which meant an annual camp in Germany every three years. A report in the *Soldier* magazine for January 1985 concerned Fusilier Thomas Thompson, aged twenty-two, of Benwell, a member of the battalion's

MT Platoon, who was praised by Northumbria Police for his action in tackling an apparently armed man who was attacking an assistant at a service station in Forest Hall. He chased and restrained the attacker until the police arrived. The weapon was found to be a replica, but Fusilier Thompson was not to know this. Police Superintendent R.P. Bensley wrote in a letter to 6/RRF, 'His actions displayed initiative and courage far beyond that which one could normally have expected from a member of the public.' Training in Germany followed in 1984, and in 1987. An addition to the battalion was the formation of the Home Service Force (HSF), located in Newcastle. This was raised from an older class of ex-servicemen for the defence of Key Points (KPs) such as communication centres, power stations, and other public utilities across the region. All this activity, the need for bigger and better facilities for the newly formed units in the North East, and the subsequent rise in the scales of equipment and vehicles held by them, led to a flurry of new building by the TA Association. Over a period of years, new TA Centres were built at Ashington: Alnwick, Cramlington – which was opened by HM Queen Elizabeth II in 1986 – Newcastle (Sandyford and Kingston Park), and Walker. Some of the old Drill Halls were either demolished, as in the case of Morpeth and the Victorian-period St Georges in Newcastle, and some were sold, like Hutton Terrace and Knightsbridge in Gosforth, to be converted into apartments.

Fusiliers of the Tyne Tees Regiment marching past the mayor of Foscani, Romania, watched by Romanian soldiers of 282 Mechanised Brigade, 2001. (J. Foster)

In the Strategic Defence Review of 1999, further reductions were made in the infantry and engineer units. On 1 April 2000, a new infantry battalion was formed. 6/RRF, 7/Light Infantry and 4/Green Howards, were disbanded and a composite battalion titled as The Tyne-Tees Regiment appeared on the Army List. It consists of two companies from the RRF: 'Z' at Ashington and 'X' in Newcastle, with detachments at Alnwick and Tynemouth. The Durham element comprises 'C' Company at Bishop Auckland, with detachments at Consett and Washington; the Teesside contribution is composed of 'B' Company at Middlesborough and a detachment at Coulby Newham; headquarters are in Durham City. The reduction of 72 Engineer Regiment to 72 (Tyne Electrical Engineers) Field Squadron (Air Support) (V), with a detachment at Sunderland, was another result of the SDR. How long this situation will prevail is anyone's guess, although events in the world today may cause a fundamental rethink with regard to the defence of the nation.

Over the years, since the start of the reforms in 1967–68, there has been a great reduction in the number of regimental bands and corps of drums. In the 1950s and 1960s, nearly every major unit in the Tyne-Tees area had a band of one sort or another. There were some excellent bands. By 2001 there were only two military bands left in the North East: The Royal Corps of Signals (TA) Band at Darlington, formerly known as 34th (Northern) Signal Regiment, which was always an excellent band, and The Northumbria Band of the Tyne-Tees Regiment based in Newcastle, which now incorporates female musicians and buglers from the former Light Infantry. This was originally the band of the old 6th (City) Battalion, RNF, which always had access to fine musicians. A factor in the loss of such bands, both military and civil, is the demise of the coal mining industry, and the loss of the colliery bands which were always a fruitful source for the TA, especially 4/5 RNF and 7/RNF, and for the artillery regiments. The Northumberland Hussars always had a superb band and highly regarded bandmasters, and in the late nineteenth century had a mounted band. Many of its members played in the once-numerous theatres in the city. They were frequent winners of the band contests held in those days. The present-day bands are continuing the high standards of musicianship that were always a hallmark of the Tyne to Tweed musicians.

A little known TA unit is 'B' Squadron, 23rd Special Air Service Regiment. This was another squadron with a BAOR role during the Cold War. With the break up of the USSR and the Warsaw Pact, other roles have been assigned to it. It is the place for self-motivated, self-reliant and confident young volunteers. The very nature of its operational role means that very little can be said about it. Other small detachments have always been part of the Territorial Army in the area. Among them today is a detachment of 25 (V) Military Intelligence Company, sited in

Colour party of the fusilier companies of the Tyne-Tees Regiment in St Nicholas Cathedral, Newcastle, April 2004. (A. Boyd)

Gateshead. A detachment of 50 Signal Squadron, 34 (Northern) Signal Regiment (V) at Heaton, Newcastle, has its headquarters in Middlesbrough. The 'Redcaps', always hovering about on large-scale exercises in the past, are represented today by No.2 Platoon, 252 Provost Company (V) Adjutant General's Corps (Royal Military Police), in Newcastle. An innovation introduced after the last SDR was that of 168 Pioneer Regiment, Royal Logistics Corps (V), with headquarters at Coulby Newham, near Middlesbrough. This regiment is composed of detachments based in many of the towns which had infantry units disbanded. Detachments can be found in Berwick-upon-Tweed, where 'C' Troop, 100 Squadron, is located. Headquarters of 100 Squadron and 'A' and 'B' Troops are situated in Cramlington. 'C' Troop of 104 Pioneer Squadron can be found at Hartlepool. In the Tyne Valley, the TA is centred on 'D' Troop of 104 Pioneer Squadron. At Tynemouth, 216 (Tyne Tees) Transport Squadron, 150 Transport Regiment Royal Logistic Corps, is based in New Clifford's Fort.

Muli-launch rocket system fired by 101 (Northumbrian) field regiment, the only TA artillery unit to be equipped with this system. (Today's TA)

Officers of the future are catered for by The Northumbrian Universities Training Corps, in a salubrious TA Centre built on what was part of the old Fenham Barracks. The artillery troop was successful in artillery competitions, winning the King George VI Challenge Cup in 1992 and 1993, as well as finishing as runners-up in 1994. As with all the other formations, The Parachute Regiment, formerly represented by 17 Parachute Battalion – the only battalion of the regiment to carry out Light Infantry drill inherited from the 9th Battalion Durham Light Infantry (TA) – from which it was formed, is now reduced to 4 Platoon, 12 Company in Hebburn as part of the 4th (Volunteer) Battalion, The Parachute Regiment, which has its sub-units scattered over a wide area. So as it will be seen, although the Territorial Army of today is much reduced numerically, there is still plenty of scope for adventurous young people to find something that suits them. However, the services are facing further reductions in their capabilities. How can those responsible justify this? Has it more to do with personal aspirations than a responsible defence strategy? But whatever the answers, there will always be those among the more responsible members of our society who will look upon it as their duty to come to the defence of our nation and defend our democratic rights, which the politically correct politicians of today seem hellbent on taking from us. These responsible citizens may even have to fight the enemy within – perhaps even against our very own politicians!

Select Bibliography

Numerous histories and accounts of the volunteers and territorials in the Tyne to Tweed area have been published over the years, especially those covering three major conflicts in which they were involved: the Boer War, the First World War and the Second World War. For instance, there are no less than seven printed histories of The Northumberland Hussars on the shelves of Newcastle Central Library. There are also newspaper accounts. Much of the information in this account has been culled from the bound volumes of newspapers held in the library, as well as in the library in North Shields; from manuscript documents held in Northumberland County Record Office; the National Archives at Kew; and the National Army Museum, London. But for those interested in the printed accounts and micro-film records in the Central Library, there is a *Volunteer Bibliography* compiled in 1998, and deposited in the local history section. If anyone knows of other local accounts and records, I would be grateful if they would inform me.

Adamson, W.; Scott, R., *The Services of the 27th Northumberland Militia, now the 3rd Battalion, Northumberland Fusiliers* (Newcastle, 1914).

Barclay, C.N., *The History of the Royal Northumberland Fusiliers in the Second World War* (London, 1952).

Beckitt, I., *The Amateur Military Tradition* (London).

Bell, J., *A Right Merry Garland of Northumberland Heroes* (Newcastle, 1814).

Bright, J., *History of the Northumberland Hussars 1924–1945* (Newcastle, 1949).

Brown, J.W., *Diary of the 1st Service Section Newcastle Royal Engineers During the Boer War 1899–1902* (Gateshead, 1904).

Cunningham, H., *The History of the Volunteer Force (A Social and Political History)* (London, 1975).

Daly, M.; Daly U., *History of the Tyne Electrical Engineers 1934–1984*, Vol.2 (Dunston, 1984).

Dennis, Peter, *The Territorial Army 1907–1940* (Woodbridge: Royal Historical Society, 1987).

Douglas, J., *A History of 272 Field Regiment R.A.(T.A.)* (typescript copy) (Newcastle, 1988).

Ed: *St George's Gazette, Regimental Journal of The Royal Northumberland Fusiliers* 1883–1968.

Fortescue, Hon. J.W., *The County Lieutenantcies and the Army 1803–1814* (London, 1909).

Hewitson, T.L., *A Volunteer Bibliography* (Newcastle, 1998).

Hewitson, T.L., *A Soldier's Life* (Newcastle, 1999).

Hewitson, T.L., *The Territorial Fusilier Company in Ashington 1903–1967* (Morpeth, 1983).

Hicks, J.G., *The Percy Artillery* (London, 1895).

Howarth, H., *Where Fate Leads* (Bolton, 1983).

Maurice-Jones, K.W., *The History of Coast Artillery in the British Army* (London, 1959).

Leathard, N.E., *34 Years with A (Hexham) Company of the 1st Volunteer Battalion, The Northumberland Fusiliers* (Hexham, 1893).

Lichfield, N.E., *The Territorial Artillery 1908–1988* (Nottingham, 1992).

Macksey, K., *The Tanks, a History of the Royal Tank Regiment 1945–1975* (London, 1979).

Ogilvie, G., *Northern Volunteers, Their Rise and Progress* (Newcastle, 1888).

Ommanney, C.H., *The History of the 1st Northumbrian Brigade, Royal Artillery (TF) 1914–1919* (Newcastle, 1927).

Pile, F., *Ack-Ack* (London, 1949).

Pease, H., *History of the Northumberland Hussars Yeomanry 1819–1925* (London, 1924).

Short, O.M.; Sherlock, R.R.; Perowne, L.E.C, *History of the Tyne Electrical Engineer R.E. 1884–1933*, Vol. 1 (Newcastle, 1935).

Swan, E.W., *The First Commission of HMS Calliope* (Newcastle, 1939).

Westlake, R., *Royal Engineers (Volunteers) 1859–1908* (Wembley, 1983).

Whittaker, J.B., *Stand Down* (Newport, 1990).

Wyrral, E., *History of the 50th Division 1914–1918* (London, 1939).

UNIT INDEX

CAVALRY:

The Bywell Volunteer Yeomanry Cavalry, 58
The Coquetdale Rangers, 45
The Imperial Yeomanry, 65
The Loyal Glendale Rangers, 47
The North Durham Yeomanry, 45
The Northumberland and Newcastle Volunteer Corps of Cavalry, 60
The Northumberland Hussars, 72
The Northumberland Hussar Yeomanry, 63
The 50th (Northumbrian) Divisional Reconnaissance Regiment (TA), 74
The Percy Tenantry Volunteer Cavalry, 49
The presentation of new Guidon, 77
The Royal Cheviot Legion, 44
The Queen's Own Yeomanry, 79
The Wallington and Kirkharle Volunteer Troop of Cavalry, 55
The 5th (York & Notts) Cavalry Brigade, 69

INFANTRY:

The Berwick Gentlemen Independent Volunteers, 51
The Corbridge Volunteer Corps of Infantry, 55
The 1st, 2nd, 4th, Volunteer Battalions, Durham Light Infantry, 97
The 2nd Hexham Rifle Volunteer Rifles, 89
The Loyal Berwick Volunteers, 51
The Morpeth Associated Volunteer Infantry, 54
The Morpeth Rifle Volunteers, 88
The Newcastle Associated Volunteer Infantry, 42

The 1st Newcastle Rifle Volunteers, 86, 92
The Newcastle Volunteer Infantry, 42
The Northern Regiment of Local Militia, 56
The North Shields and Tynemouth Volunteer Infantry, 56
The 1st Northumberland and Berwick-upon-Tweed Rifle Volunteers, 91
The 1st Northumberland Volunteers, 84
The 1st Volunteer Battalion, The Northumberland Fusiliers, 91
The 2nd Volunteer Battalion, The Northumberland Fusiliers, 92
The 3rd Volunteer Battalion, The Northumberland Fusiliers, 92
The 3rd (Militia) Battalion, Northumberland Fusiliers, 31
The 5th (Militia) Battalion, Northumberland Fusiliers, 32
The Northumberland Light Infantry Militia, 24
The Northumberland Militia, 15
The Percy Tenantry Volunteer Infantry, 47
The Royal Cheviot Legion Infantry, 44
The Seaton Delaval Associated Corps of Volunteers, 53
The Southern Regiment of Local Militia, 57
The Tyne and Tees Brigade, 97
The 1st Tyneside Volunteers, 91
The Wallsend Volunteer Rifle Corps, 56
The 8th Walker Rifle Volunteers, 91
The Western Regiment of Local Militia, 56

ARTILLERY:

The 1st Berwick-on-Tweed Artillery Volunteers, 109
The 3rd Blyth & Cowpen Artillery Volunteers, 103
The 3rd Durham Artillery Volunteers, 105
The 'Elswick Battery', 111
The 1st Newcastle Artillery Volunteers, 90, 105
The 3rd Brigade, Northern Division, R.A., 110
The Northumberland Artillery Militia, 38-40
The 1st Northumberland Artillery Volunteers, 102, 105
The 3rd Northumberland Artillery Volunteers, 88, 103
The 2nd Northumberland (Percy) Artillery Volunteers, 107
The 1st Northumbrian Brigade RFA (TF), 129
The 101 (Northumbrian) Field Regiment RA (V), 179
The Royal Artillery (TA) amalgamations, 164,166, 173
The Tynemouth Royal Garrison Artillery, 129

ENGINEERS:

The Coast Battalion, Royal Engineers, 117, 119
The Coastal Defence Battalion, Royal Engineers, 121
composition of 72 Engineer Regiment, 178
The Tyne Division Royal Engineer (Volunteers) Electrical Engineers, 122
The Tyne Division Royal Engineer (Volunteers) Submarine Miners, 117
The 1st Durham (Durham & Newcastle upon Tyne) Corps, 115
The 1st Durham Engineer (Volunteers), 116
29 Engineer Brigade, 178
72 Engineer Regiment, 178
The Newcastle & Durham Engineer (Volunteers), 116
The 1st Newcastle upon Tyne & Durham Corp, Royal Engineers (Volunteers), 115
The Northumberland Divisional Royal Engineers, 130
Amalgamation of Royal Engineer units, 174
The Tyne Electrical Engineers, Royal Engineers, 130
Tyne Electrical (Fortress) Royal Engineers, 141

LOGISTICS:

The Northumberland Brigade Company, Royal Army Service Corps, 130
The Northumbrian Divisional Casualty Clearing Station, Royal Army Medical Corps, 130
The Northumbrian Divisional Section, Army Veterinary Corps, 130, 166
The Northumbrian Divisional Veterinary Hospital, Army Veterinary Corps, 130
The 1st Northumbrian Field Ambulance, Royal Army Medical Corps, 130
149 Field Ambulance, Royal Army Medical Corps, (TAVR), 175
201 (Northern) General Hospital, Royal Army Medical Corps (TAVR), 175
552 (General Transport) Company, Royal Army Service Corps, (TA), 166

If you are interested in purchasing other books published by Tempus,
or in case you have difficulty finding any Tempus books in your local bookshop,
you can also place orders directly through our website

www.tempus-publishing.com